8.75

GEORGE ELIOT
and her world

MARGHANITA LASKI

GEORGE ELIOT

and her world

THAMES AND HUDSON
LONDON

Frontispiece: George Eliot in 1860, from a drawing in chalks by Samuel Laurence.

Printed in Great Britain by
Jarrold and Sons Ltd Norwich
ISBN 0 500 13043 4

'IT IS TOO MUCH TO HOPE that no member of her own family will figure in it,' Mrs Fanny Houghton wrote to her half-brother Isaac Evans, George Eliot's own brother, when *Felix Holt* was announced in 1866. Fanny's worry was understandable. In almost all George Eliot's works of fiction so far, family, friends and acquaintances had felt able to identify characters, places and events as taken from the author's own life and experiences, and to such an extent that every biographer has to decide how far George Eliot's fiction may be treated as source material for her life.

But George Eliot herself almost always denied, vehemently and with distress, the validity of such apparent likenesses. And at least for this reason it seems proper to approach her life from the standpoint of facts that can be independently established, and to consider possible fictional evidence as it arises.

It was believed in the Evans family that they descended from a sixteenth-century Welsh knight, Sir Thomas Evans de Northop, in the County of Flint, and from Northop they almost certainly came. By the late seventeenth century they were established in the parish of Norbury in Derbyshire, a possible ancestor of George Eliot being an Evans described in the parish register as 'Joseph Evans, a traveller', or tramp. In the next century her grandfather, George Evans (1740–1830), the village carpenter, wheelwright and undertaker, was living and working in a small plain cottage, still standing at Roston Common, Norbury. He and his wife, Mary Leach (1738–1803), had eight children, five sons and three daughters. The eldest son, George

The cottage at Roston Common, Norbury, where Robert Evans was born.

(*Opposite*) Map of Warwickshire, 1852, with sketch below showing Midlands associations with George Eliot.

5

'I set this morning for my likeness to be taken.' (Robert Evans's *Diary*, 11 July 1842). The miniature by Carlisle.

(b. 1766), soon went off to near-by Rocester, drank heavily and died young. The four younger sons, William (b. 1769), Thomas (b. 1771), Robert, George Eliot's father (b. 1773), and Samuel (b. 1777), after limited but adequate village schooling, began their working lives in their father's trade. Robert, eventually followed by the rest of the family, soon crossed the boundary river Dove and set up in the village of Ellastone in Staffordshire.

There were then three 'great houses' based on Ellastone, and one of them, Wootton Hall, was owned by the Davenport family of Cheshire (see p. 118) In 1766 Wootton Hall had been let, at a charitably nominal rent, to an eccentric Frenchman who wore Armenian dress, and was long remembered locally as 'Owd Rossall'. This was Jean-Jacques Rousseau, aged fifty-four, seeking refuge with his companion Thérèse Levasseur. At first Rousseau was delighted with the landscape and the solitude, and with the grotto where he began to write his *Confessions*. But after a year he had become convinced that the servants were poisoning him, and fled.

Before Robert Evans moved to Ellastone, Wootton Hall had been let to Francis Parker, whose wife was a sister of the then Davenport owner. When Francis Parker later inherited Newdigate property at Kirk Hallam in Derbyshire, he took the name and arms of Newdigate, and as Newdigate it is convenient to know him from the start. He will be called here Francis I to distinguish him from his son, Francis II, born in 1774 and so a year younger than Robert Evans.

It is said that the two young men, Robert Evans and Francis Newdigate II, became close friends, and that it was through this friendship that Robert Evans was employed on the Wootton Hall estate, first as forester, later as estate bailiff. It is not clear whether he was employed by the Davenports or directly by Francis Newdigate I, but it was as a result of this employment that his substantial talents gradually became fully extended. What they were, George Eliot described in a letter of 30 September 1859:

– my Father . . . raised himself from being an artizan to be a man whose extensive knowledge in very varied practical departments made his services valued through several counties. He had large knowledge of building, of mines, of plantations, of various branches of valuation and measurement – of all that is essential to the management of large estates. He was held by those competent to judge as *unique* amongst land-agents for his manifold knowledge and experience, which enabled him to save the special fees usually paid by landowners for special opinions on the different questions incident to the proprietorship of land.

It was said, too, that he was immensely strong, could pick up and carry beams too heavy for young apprentices; that he could judge to a nicety the timber any tree would provide; and that he was scrupulously honest. His immense range of practical knowledge must have been gained empirically and over years. His diaries show that his literacy, though adequate, was less than conventional, but of his great abilities there can be no doubt.

The Newdigates provided not only Robert Evans's first step on the ladder of a successful career, but also, it seems, his first wife. Harriet Poynton, according to the record of marriage on 27 May 1801 in the Ellastone Church parish register, was a local girl, apparently employed at the Hall.

6

Wootton Hall, Staffordshire, rented by Francis Parker (later Parker-Newdigate – Francis I) from the Davenport family.

Soon after, life changed for the Parker-Newdigates and for the Evans family too. In 1802, when Francis I inherited his property at Kirk Hallam, between Nottingham and Derby, Robert Evans moved there to manage it. The pretty house at Ellastone and the carpenter's business were taken over by his brother William, who became a substantial builder, and the estate business by Thomas. Samuel, in 1795, had been converted from the family's conventional Anglicanism to Methodism, and thereafter placed his religious duties first; he was, said his biographer, 'too yielding and too confiding to be entrusted with the affairs of this world'. In 1804 he married Elizabeth Tomlinson, a lace-mender from Nottingham who had herself been converted to Methodism in 1797 and was locally known as a preacher. In 1807 Samuel left the family business and eventually settled in a four-roomed stone cottage outside Wirksworth, some twelve miles north of Derby, where he managed the Harlaam lace-works, and husband and wife, with their three children, led devoutly religious lives.

Of Robert Evans's children by his first marriage, Robert was born at Ellastone in 1802, and Frances Lucy, known as Fanny, at Kirk Hallam in 1805. Robert had bought a farm there which he worked on his own account. The Parker-Newdigates did not move to the family house at West Hallam, but they were soon called from Ellastone to other duties.

From 1734 the head of their family had been Sir Roger Newdigate of Harefield, Middlesex and Arbury Hall, Warwickshire, fifth – and last – baronet, and founder of the Newdigate Prize at Oxford. (There were to

7

Arbury Hall, Warwickshire, once an Augustinian monastery, since 1586 the principal seat of the Newdigate family. In the latter half of the eighteenth century Sir Roger Newdigate substantially rebuilt the Hall in the Gothic style. It was the model for 'Cheverel Manor...the castellated house of grey-tinted stone' of *Mr Gilfil's Love-Story*.

(*Below*) Arbury Farm, later called South Farm. George Eliot's birthplace.

be no compliments to him in the Prize Poem, he said – 'if there is, it will make me sick' – and not more than fifty lines – 'I won't tire them in the Theatre.') He lived at Arbury, the family seat since the sixteenth century, and married twice, his second wife, Hester Mundy, in 1776. There were no children of either marriage. Through his mother, Francis I was Sir Roger's nearest kinsman, and he and his son would be expected to have succeeded to the property, but for some period before 1795 Charles Parker, his younger brother, had apparently been regarded as the heir. But this Charles – Charles I – died in that year with his only son an infant, and Sir Roger's will of 1800 left his estates to Francis I for life, and thereafter to Charles I's son, Charles II, and his heirs, requesting them to take the family name in its older form Newdegate. The second Lady Newdigate died in 1800, and some little time later, probably in 1804, Francis I and his wife moved to Arbury. Sir Roger died in 1806 in his eighty-seventh year.

Francis Parker-Newdigate (Francis I), Robert Evans's employer.

There was now a very great estate to be managed, and Francis I sent for Robert Evans. Thomas Evans took over the management of the Kirk Hallam estates, and rented Robert's farm there, William taking on the Wootton Hall management, presumably under the Davenports. Robert Evan's dwellings were always singularly attractive ones, and his first home in Warwickshire was Arbury Farm, now South Farm, in the parish of Astley, which was and is a pleasant working farmhouse. In 1809 his wife Harriet died; a memorial tablet to her in Astley Church describes her as 'for many years the friend and servant of the family at Arbury'. In 1813 he married Christiana Pearson (born in 1788).

This was generally considered a socially superior marriage for Robert, in that the Pearson family was, in a small way, a locally substantial one. Christiana's father was Constable for Astley parish and a churchwarden, and her brother Isaac a farmer and grazier at Fillongley. Of Christiana's three sisters, Elizabeth was married to Richard Johnson of Bulkington, Ann to John Garner of Fillongley, and Mary was the second wife of John Evarard of Attleborough, then a village just outside Nuneaton. The Pearson influence is apparent in the names given to the children born of this marriage, in 1814 Christiana Pearson (for her mother), in 1816 Isaac Pearson (for his maternal grandfather and maternal uncle) and on 22 November, St Cecilia's Day, 1819, at five o'clock in the morning, Mary Ann, named for two of the Pearson aunts.

She was called by many names in her life; Marianne, Polly, Pollian, Marian, Minie, Mater, Mutter, Madonna, and, of course, George Eliot. She was christened Mary Anne but her father, recording her birth, wrote Mary Ann in his diary. In the parish register he described himself as 'farmer' which would not have pleased his daughter; her letter, quoted above, was an angry response to hearing she had been described as a 'self-educated farmer's daughter', and the passage begins, 'my Father did not raise himself from being an artizan to be a farmer; he raised himself from being an artizan to be a man . . .'.

Mary Ann's christening was at Chilvers Coton parish church. The family moved from Astley to that parish a few months after her birth, to

Chilvers Coton church before its bombing in the Second World War, yet already 'improved' from 'Shepperton Church as it was in the old days, with its outer coat of rough stucco, its red-tiled roof, its hetero-geneous windows patched with desultory bits of painted glass –' (*Amos Barton*, Ch. I).

George Eliot's baptismal certificate in Chilvers Coton church. 'Mary Ann Evans was born at Arbury Farm, at five o'clock this morning.' (Robert Evans's *Journal*, 22 November 1819.)

another Newdigate property, the far more substantial Griff House on the Coventry–Nuneaton road. It, like South Farm, remains much as it then was, though the adjacent motorway network is making it less pleasantly habitable than it was in the 1820s, when it was a delight to look out for the two stage-coaches, to and from Stamford and Birmingham, that passed it each day. Since then, the dairy has been incoporated into the house and the garden pond has nearly dried up. The bow-window still juts from the elegant drawing-room, and the wide dignified staircase to the first floor gives way to a steep climb to the large empty attics, once Mary Ann's retreat in loneliness or distress.

Griff House – 'My old, old home' (G.E. *Letters*, 5 December 1859). 'I seem to feel the air through the window of the attic above the drawing room, from which, when a little girl, I often looked towards the distant view of the Coton "College"' (G.E. *Letters*, 9 May 1874). 'This attic was Maggie's favourite retreat …here she fretted out all her ill-humours, and talked aloud to the worm-eaten floors and the worm-eaten shelves, and the dark rafters festooned with cobwebs.' (*The Mill on the Floss*, Ch. IV.)

The dining-room at Arbury Hall:
'–that dining-room . . . impressed one
with its architectural beauty like a
cathedral . . . the lofty groined ceiling,
with its richly-carved pendants, all a
creamy white, relieved here and there by
touches of gold–' (*Mr Gilfil's Love-
Story*, Ch. II).

The housekeeper's room at Arbury
Hall which George Eliot reproduced
in *Mr Gilfil's Love-Story*, only chang-
ing the motto over the fireplace from
TRUSTE IN GOD AND FEARE HIM
WITH AL THY HARTE to FEAR GOD
AND HONOUR THE KING.

Each of the three younger children was somebody's favourite, tidy composed Chrissey the favourite of the aunts, Isaac of his sharp-tongued competent mother, and Mary Ann of her father. He would take her up to Arbury Hall, leaving her in the housekeeper's room while he transacted his business. When going round the countryside, he would take her with him, wedged firmly between his knees, in the gig, and once at least to Derbyshire and Staffordshire. Robert Evans's own work was taking him far afield, for his competence had led to his being regularly consulted by other landowners, whose names are variously given. They certainly included Lord Aylesford of Packington. Mr Bromley-Davenport is also mentioned, which is interesting if confusing, since the name did not exist in that form until 1868; but we may suppose that through the Davenport connection Robert Evans was employed by the Bromleys of Baginton, and after 1822, by the Reverend Walter Davenport Bromley who then became owner of Baginton as well as of Wootton Hall. Perhaps it was for him that both the younger Robert and Isaac named sons Walter – not a Pearson or Evans family name.

The Rev. Walter Davenport Bromley, with his wife and pug-dog, in the drawing-room of Wootton Hall.

13

The Griff Canal.

Our brown canal was endless to my thought;
And on its banks I sat in dreamy peace—

(from G.E.'s sonnet sequence,
Brother and Sister).

Apart from her father whom she always loved dearly, Mary Ann's devotion was given to her brother Isaac, who returned it with only an older brother's rough critical affection. By her own admission, the childhood of Tom and Maggie Tulliver recalls the relationship, and her sonnet sequence 'Brother and Sister' (1874) is frankly autobiographical. In these sonnets we read of the little sister neglecting dolls for her brother's marbles and humming-tops, and of fishing in the canal – the Griff Canal built by Sir Roger to carry away the Arbury coal. Water, for pleasure and pain, was to be a potent image in George Eliot's novels.

Mary Ann was never pretty, even as a child. She was clumsy, with an overlarge head, subject to rages and fits of weeping; she could never sit easy to life. But she had her pretensions, and when only four would sit at the piano pretending to play, in order to impress the servants.

Piano-playing was soon to be only one of many accomplishments. Mr and Mrs Evans cared for their children's betterment, and they all received good educations. Chrissey was early sent to boarding-school while Isaac and Mary Ann went to Mrs Moore's dame school, then just outside Griff House. But the children were getting to be too much for Mrs Evans, pulled down after the birth of twins, William and Thomas (Evans family names, this time), in 1821; they died at ten days old. In 1824 Isaac was sent to school at

14

Foleshill, a couple of miles the Nuneaton side of Coventry, and Mary Ann, aged five, joined Chrissey at Miss Lathom's school at Attleborough, where Aunt Evarard lived, which was pleasant for Chrissey but small consolation for Mary Ann, homesick, chronically cold, and beset with night terrors.

She lived for the holidays and the chance of seeing Isaac again; but Isaac was growing away from her, and not least because he now had a pony. Mary Ann was always frightened of horses, never willingly mounting even a donkey, and always nervous when driven. (When it came to *Daniel Deronda*, the publisher had to explain that a horse which stumbled on grass would be unlikely to break its knees.) Robert Evans was perhaps not over-fond of riding himself; when Queen Adelaide came to Nuneaton in 1839 and was escorted there from Griff by the tenants, the cavalcade went, he wrote in his diary, 'faster than I liked to ride'.

Mary Ann had been a late reader, preferring to play with Isaac, but now she turned to reading for consolation, often, to her mother's annoyance, in bed. Her first book, a present from her father called *The Linnet's Life*, she kept till her death. At home she read the then usual library of even non-bookish households, *Pilgrim's Progress*, *The Vicar of Wakefield*, *Aesop's Fables*, which still in later life would elicit her infrequent bursts of laughter, and, of course, the Bible and soon the works of Shakespeare; these last two became part of her own language. She read *Rasselas* and Defoe's *History of the Devil* and the then widely popular compendium *Joe Miller's Jest Book* from which she was apt, often disconcertingly, to quote. Then in 1827, through a neighbour's loan to Chrissey, she was introduced to Sir Walter Scott, who was long to influence her. The book was *Waverley*, returned to the lender before Mary Ann could finish it, and her distress so much affected the elders that she was given a copy for herself.

Despite her dolefulness, Mary Ann was not unpopular at Miss Latham's school. The older girls made a pet of her, calling her Little Mama, but were careful, in their romping, not to dishevel her, for she didn't like to be made untidy; it was there that, like Maggie Tulliver, she cut off her curls, enraged that they wouldn't be disciplined. But Mary Ann did not care for contemporaries; 'I like to talk to grown-up people,' she explained, when found sitting alone at a children's party.

Her next school, to which she was sent in 1828, was more to her taste. The Elms in Church Lane (now Vicarage Street), Nuneaton, was run by widowed Mrs John Wallington, with Miss Maria Lewis the principal governess for the thirty-odd boarders. Miss Lewis was an Irishwoman, a devoted Evangelical, and for many years a major influence in Mary Ann's life, setting her religious opinions in a stricter mould than that of her easy-going conventional family, and arousing her intellectual curiosity and ever-increasing desire to learn. Old schoolfellows later described Mary Ann as a quiet reserved girl, with strongly lined, almost masculine features. When she stood up in class her features, heavy in repose, were lightened by eager excitement, which found further vent in nervous movements of the hands.

At the Elms, Mary Ann learned English and drawing and some French, and began to be proficient at the piano. By the age of thirteen it was felt she

'When she stood up in the class her features, heavy in repose, were lighted by eager excitement, which found further vent in nervous movements of her hands.' A contemporary's recollection of Mary Ann Evans in the schoolroom of The Elms, Nuneaton, shown here (reported in the *Graphic*, 8 January 1881).

had learned all that Mrs Wallington's school could teach, and her parents were advised to send her to the Misses Franklin's school in Coventry. But for years yet she was to remain under the influence of Maria Lewis, who constantly corresponded with her, and visited Griff in the holidays.

Nantglyn, Warwick Row, where Mary and Rebecca Franklin kept school, was in the best part of Coventry. The Misses Franklin were themselves of comparatively simple origin, daughters of Francis Franklin, the Minister of Cow Lane Baptist Chapel. When Mary Ann went to Nantglyn, they were still in their twenties, Mary, who had served her apprenticeship in teaching in Essex, 'motherly, warm-hearted, businesslike', Rebecca, who (like Esther Lyon of *Felix Holt*) had had a year in Paris, providing lofty elegance. Perhaps the greatest gift Miss Rebecca gave to Mary Ann was her voice. Robert Evans's was a country voice that lapsed into broad Staffordshire, and Mrs Evans, though more 'refined', must have had a marked provincial accent. Indeed, though Maria Edgeworth was socially contemptuous of provincial accents, these cannot have been uncommon even among educated people. Boys as well as girls were still often educated only locally or at home, and around the middle of the nineteenth century we do not find provincial accents adduced as criteria of social status, though lower-class London accents may be unkindly remarked upon.

But thanks to Miss Rebecca's example and training Mary Ann lost her original speech patterns, acquired a lasting habit of speaking in perfectly made sentences, and developed the beautiful deep voice (deeper still when she was moved) that was to impress everyone who met her. She gained much in conventional education too. The regular school courses comprised English, French, history, arithmetic, drawing, and music taught by Edward Simms,

excellent education

the organist of St Michael's Church. Mary Ann became so deft at the piano that she was often asked to perform for visitors, an experience agonizing to her shyness and usually followed by bursts of tears in her bedroom. Music was not yet the passion it was to become: as late as 1838 she was writing to Maria Lewis of a concert in Coventry.

'I am not fitted to decide on the question of the propriety or lawfulness of such exhibitions of talent and so forth because I have no soul for music . . . it would not cost me any regrets if the only music heard in our land were that of strict worship.'

In French, Mary Ann excelled, winning, at the age of thirteen, a copy of Pascal's *Pensées*. She was also outstanding at English composition. A notebook she kept at school still exists, with the name Marianne Evans on the first page; she was evidently, like many schoolgirls, fancifying her name. In it, with mathematical exercises, copied poems, and a pompous essay 'Affectation and Conceit', is her first known fiction, the beginnings of a heavily derivative and sadly anachronistic historical romance of the Commonwealth period, named by G. S. Haight, after its hero, *Edward Neville*.

At Nantglyn, new religious influences weighed on Mary Ann. The girls went to services at Mr Franklin's chapel, and to Miss Lewis's pious yet gentle Evangelicanism was added sterner nonconformity, with stress on hell-fire and the need to be saved. Mary Ann responded by the practice of such austerities as wearing a peculiarly unbecoming cap in token of renunciation of the world's vanities, and especially mortifying to a girl already aware of her own ugliness; a visitor to the school, to whom she had opened the door, took her, at the age of thirteen, for one of the Misses Franklin. Her new religious views contributed to the widening gulf between herself and Isaac. He had been sent

Of Mary Ann's years at Nantglyn School, Coventry (*above*), a fellow pupil recalled that 'Her schoolfellows loved her as much as they could venture to love one whom they felt so immeasurably superior to themselves', and added that a source of great interest and envy to the girls was 'the weekly cart which brought Miss Evans new-laid eggs and other delightful produce of her father's farm'.

to a private tutor called Docker near Birmingham, and Docker's influence not only confirmed Isaac's inclination to all conventional acceptances but steered his religious sympathies towards High Church views and, later, Tractarianism. He could have little in common with a sister who read Paley's *Evidences* and led the school prayer-meetings.

Though there was good will, there was at this time little contact between the children of the first marriage and those of the second. The younger Robert had been trained to his father's trade, and already by the year of Mary Ann's birth, when he was seventeen, had been sent to the Kirk Hallam estates under his father and, presumably, his uncle Thomas. Fanny went too, to housekeep for Robert, and, it is said, to teach the children of the Parker family there. Possibly she went to Kirk Hallam after Robert or came home more often, for she and Mary Ann for some time retained an affectionate relationship. And when Robert died in 1864, in a period of minimal contact with her own family, Mary Ann wrote to Robert's son of his 'unbroken kindness and generous brotherliness' to her, and to his widow that 'I remember nothing earlier than the knowledge that I had a brother Robert.' Robert had married Jane Attenborough, and had seven children, of whom one son was to be knighted. Fanny, who outlived Mary Ann, married Henry Houghton (pronounced Hooton) of Baginton.

Mary Ann left school at Christmas 1835, the first Christmas she received the sacrament. For a short time the family were together at Griff, but the next year was to be one of loss. It opened with Robert Evans suffering painfully from an attack of kidney stone. After leeches and bleedings he began slowly to recover, but, as January wore on, Mrs Evans's now chronic ill-health deteriorated. By the end of the month she was in acute pain, with her legs paralysed. William Bucknill, their Nuneaton surgeon, had to warn the family there was no hope, and on 3 February 1836 Christiana Evans died.

For a little over a year Chrissey and Mary Ann kept house together for their father, Chrissey busied with the more domestic chores, Mary Ann trying to fill her mother's place with advice and companionship, and, in the evenings, reading Scott's novels aloud, as her father liked her to do until his death. But in May 1837 Chrissey married Edward Clarke, a surgeon at Meriden, some five miles west of Coventry. Mary Ann was bridesmaid, and received as bridesmaid's gifts a pocket prayer-book and a book of Sunday Lessons.

Now, though there were servants for the menial tasks, all the work of running the home fell on Mary Ann. Hers was the responsibility for putting up the preserves in season and of preparing for the Michaelmas Harvest Home, festivities whose coarseness she found 'nauseating'. The dairy too was her responsibility, and in later years she would show a right hand larger than the left, from, she maintained, years of cheese-making. (But Isaac, when he heard these stories, pooh-poohed them, and said that Mary Ann would never have anything to do with cheese-making.) In those days Mary Ann was disturbed by poverty, guilty at her own plenty 'while the haggard looks and piercing glance of want and conscious hopelessness are to be seen in the streets', as she wrote to Miss Lewis. She organized a local clothing club and was active in other such charitable works of small village gentry, as the Evanses must now be counted – as executor to Aunt Evarard's will of 1840, Isaac was described as 'gentleman'. But her mind was not quiescent or her education ended. Signor Brezzi came from Coventry to teach her German, French and Italian, and she read Greek and Latin with the Reverend Thomas Sheepshanks, Headmaster of Coventry Free Grammar School. Her religious feelings were ever more tending to Evangelical strictness, and her letters to Maria Lewis were heavy with pompous piety. She must have been sad company for Isaac when he came home from hunting or his day's work at his father's trade. When she visited London with him in 1838 she refused to accompany him to the theatre and instead sat at home reading Josephus's *History of the Jews*. 'I used to go about like an owl, to the great disgust of my brother, and I would have denied him what I see now to have been quite lawful amusements,' she said later.

At this period, as ever thereafter, she was reading deeply and widely, and above all in theology. The so-called 'secondary squire' of Chilvers Coton, Henry Harpur of Caldwell Hall, lent her books, principally of a Tractarian trend, hoping, Mary Ann wrote of one such, 'to make me a proselyte to the opinions it advocates'. And she had the run of the Arbury Hall Library.

'The library lay but three steps from the dining-room...the flat heavily-carved ceiling, and the dark hue of the old books that lined the walls, made the room look sombre–' George Eliot's description in *Mr Gilfil's Love-Story* of the Cheverel Manor library based on the library of Arbury Hall (*below*).

'I had entirely done with the pleasures of the world, and with all my old companions...I pulled off all my bunches–cut off my curls–and in this I found an unspeakable pleasure.' This account of the conversion to Methodism of Elizabeth Tomlinson, who married Samuel Evans, was written in her own hand; her portrait and a specimen of her handwriting are seen above.

(*Opposite*) The house at Foleshill. On 19 March 1841, Robert Evans recorded in his *Journal* that when he told Lord Aylesford that 'I was going to my new residence this evening for the first night, on the Foleshill road in Coventry parish, he Laphd and said they would make me Mayor.'

There had been changes at the Hall. Charles Newdigate Parker Newdegate – Charles II – died in 1833, and in 1835, when Francis I died, it was Charles II's son, Charles Newdigate-Newdegate, the grandson of Sir Roger's original heir, who inherited, at the age of nineteen. He never married. 'Filial affection and his devotion to public life had, no doubt, much to do with his denying himself the married state,' said his obituary in the *Nuneaton Chronicle* in 1887, and it was his mother who invited Mary Ann to use the library so that she could work on a project she conceived in 1839, a Chart of Ecclesiastical History; fortunately, someone else published something similar before it was finished. Mary Ann had, however, come to consider publication a proper fruit of work, and her first published piece, a religious poem signed M.A.E., appeared in the *Christian Observer* of January 1840 with an editorial note on some dubious theology in one verse.

In 1839 Uncle and Aunt Samuel Evans visited Griff, and it is said to have been on that occasion that Elizabeth Evans told her niece how in 1802 she and another pious woman, a Miss Richards, had spent the night in the condemned cell at Nottingham Jail with Mary Voce, who was hanged next morning for child murder. At this time Mary Ann was deeply impressed with her aunt's piety, though it was of a gentler kind than her own stern near-Calvinism. She corresponded with the Samuel Evanses when they went home to Wirksworth. Elizabeth sent devotional books and was thanked for her 'welcome and valuable letters', though in 1859, when accused of taking Dinah Morris's sermons in *Adam Bede* from her aunt's sermon notes, Mary Ann declared she had never seen anything of her aunt's writing. The following June, in 1840, a return visit was paid by Robert Evans and Mary Ann, and on this occasion, Elizabeth's family and neighbours later maintained, Mary Ann came with a notebook in which she recorded long conversations with her aunt; but this too she denied. In September, Mary Ann went with Isaac to Edgbaston to visit Isaac's future wife, Sarah Rawlins, daughter of a Birmingham hide merchant who was an old friend of Robert Evans's. Mary Ann had begun to enjoy music and at Birmingham she confessed to pleasure in hearing the *Messiah*.

With a new master at Arbury Hall, with Isaac about to marry and suf-
ficiently competent in his profession, Robert Evans, now nearing his seventies,
was ready to retire from active work, though he retained a partnership with
Isaac and still saw clients. Had he followed his own inclinations he would
have moved to a cottage at Packington that he rented from Lord Aylesford.
But there was Mary Ann to be thought of, twenty-two years old and with, as
yet, no matrimonial prospects, though someone, referred to as 'the beloved
object' in a letter to Maria Lewis of April 1840, had touched her heart, and she
was certainly, as for many years to come, ripe for almost any man who should
show an interest in her. She confessed to Miss Lewis that she found her
language teacher, Joseph Brezzi, 'anything but uninteresting, all external
grace and mental power'. But she feared that 'the bliss of reciprocated affection' was not to be hers.

Her family feared this too, but they were determined to give her every
chance, and Robert Evans's next and last home was his grandest. Later
known as Bird Grove, it was in Foleshill, just off the Coventry–Nuneaton
main road and five minutes' walk into Coventry, a town then principally
dependent on ribbon-manufacture with some 30,000 inhabitants. Consisting
at that time of two semi-detached dwellings, the whole something more than a
villa, less than a mansion, the Foleshill house still has dignity, though half has
been demolished, the elegant roof-balustrades removed, and, in place of surrounding fields, there are now little red-brick houses. Robert Evans and Mary
Ann removed there in March 1841 at, Robert's diary noted, considerable
expense: £254 19s 6d for new furniture alone. In June, Isaac married Sarah
at Edgbaston.

Silhouette of George Eliot as a girl.

The drawing-room at Foleshill: 'the window curtains, Blinds, and the Carpiting on the Dining-room and Drawing-room floors' were, Robert Evans's *Journal* noted, taken with the house, as well as nearly £100 worth of the previous tenant's furniture.

Mary Ann and her father already had many acquaintances in Coventry. The Misses Franklin, still schoolkeeping, introduced the Evanses to their own circle of friends, of whom the most important to Mary Ann were to be the Sibrees (pronounced Sigh-bree). John Sibree, Minister of the Independent Chapel in Vicar Lane, had two children, John, who had been to a German university and was intended for the Church, and Mary, then sixteen, who developed for Mary Ann that adoration she was constantly to receive from women. Then Mary Ann was continuing with her lessons, and the Reverend Thomas Sheepshanks was friend of the family as well as tutor, though the Evanses did not attend his church, St John's, but went to Trinity Church in the centre of Coventry. Its Vicar, John Howells, who owned the lease of the Foleshill house, was tinged by Evangelicalism, but not so enthusiastically as to offend Robert Evans, who was proud to take round the collection-plate.

Mary Ann was reading ever more deeply and widely, in theology, in French and German literature, and now in the Romantics too, with especial and lasting devotion to Wordsworth. The Arbury Hall library was no longer available. The Newdigates and their ramifications had seemingly passed out of her life, and only the future was to show how powerfully they had impressed themselves upon it. In fact, by the time that Mary Ann left Griff House, she had amassed all the material for George Eliot's earlier novels and much that was to serve her right up to the last one.

Still, she was not short of books. What couldn't be found in Coventry, Maria Lewis could buy and post from London, where she was now working. And as she read, Mary Ann's religious views were changing, at first, perhaps,

Caroline (Cara) Hennell (1814–1905); a miniature painted in 1833 by her sister Sara. The youngest of the eight children of James Hennell, a commercial traveller and strict Unitarian, Cara married the free-thinking Charles Bray in 1836.

unrealized by herself, and certainly unknown to those around her when she first met the neighbours in the adjoining house, Mr and Mrs Abijah Hill Pears. Mr Pears was a ribbon-manufacturer and in 1842–43, Mayor of Coventry; his wife was the sister of Charles Bray.

When he first met Mary Ann in November 1841, Charles Bray was thirty and already known — in Coventry even notorious – for his progressive views. Son of a ribbon-manufacturer, he had been since 1835 established in Coventry's traditional trade, and his views and actions were already unconventional in early manhood when he set up an infants' school in a poor neighbourhood and promoted an unsectarian school for dissenters. In the 1830s he wrote much on education, and *The Education of the Feelings*, first published in 1838, reached its last edition as late as 1872; but his best-known work was *The Philosophy of Necessity* of 1841, which gave an historical outline of communities founded on the principle of co-operation. In 1836 he had married Caroline Hennell, known as Cara, and sought to convert her from Unitarianism to his own non-religious views. She, in perplexity, consulted her Unitarian brother Charles who, after two years of study, published in 1838 *An Inquiry Concerning the Origin of Christianity*, in which he concluded that Christianity could not be accepted as stemming from Divine Revelation, but that it was 'the purest form yet existing of natural religion'. To Mary Ann this book was to be seminal.

In 1840 Bray had bought Rosehill, a property in St Nicholas Street, Radford, on the outskirts of Coventry. He described it in his autobiography, *Phases of Opinion and Experience during a Long Life*, published in 1884:

'–that wooded retreat, far enough from the town for country quiet, and yet near enough to hear the sweet church bells and the chimes of St. Michael's–' Charles Bray, of his house Rosehill (*above*).

a house with large lawn shaded by noble groups of trees, and especially by a fine old acacia, the sloping turf about whose roots made a delightful seat in summer time. We spread there a large bear-skin, and many friends have enjoyed a seat there in that wooden retreat. . . . There was a free-and-easy mental atmosphere, harmonizing with the absence of all pretension and conventionality, which I believe gave a peculiar charm to this modest residence . . . everyone who came to Coventry with a queer mission, or a crochet, or was supposed to be a 'little cracked', was sent up to Rosehill.

But it was not because Mary Ann was a little cracked that she was sent there. It was because the Pears hoped that her known piety might work upon Bray's scepticism.

In the event, it was to be not so much the other way round as an explosion of like-mindedness, the revelation to Mary Ann of an ambience in which the doubts that had been fermenting could finally be resolved. Meeting Charles Bray, encountering the atmosphere of his home, the conversation of his visitors, was for Mary Ann an *Italienische Reise*, a fulminant release. On Sunday, 2 January 1842, Robert Evans's diary contained the entry, 'Went to Trinity Church in the forenoon . . . Mary Ann did not go'.

In later years, the outrage caused by Mary Ann's refusal to go to church would have shocked her profoundly. No one was to be more conventional than Mrs George Henry Lewes. In retrospect, it seems that this present act of infidelity outraged her family more than anything she was to do thereafter. Contact with the Samuel Evanses was permanently broken; Elizabeth Evans's granddaughter remembered that in her childhood her mother would present Mary Ann as 'an example of all that was wicked'. Some eighty years

afterwards a Staffordshire cousin, William Mottram, recalled that in Ellastone she was considered a person 'whose delinquency was an aggravated kind'. Robert Evans refused to speak to his daughter and began making plans to break up the Foleshill establishment and move alone to the cottage at Packington. Friends were brought in to mediate. John Sibree spent an evening in hard but fruitless argument. He then produced a Professor of Theology from Birmingham, Francis Watts, who could only conclude, 'She has gone into the question.' The Misses Franklin brought forward a Baptist minister, who reported, 'That young lady must have had the devil at her elbow to suggest her doubts, for there was not a book that I recommended to her in support of Christian evidences that she had not read.' Sisters and brother brought tact to bear, Chrissey took Mary Ann off to Meriden, Fanny counselled moderation and outward compliance. Isaac was as angry as his father, especially in view of likely harm to Mary Ann's matrimonial chances, but he behaved sensibly. After an appealing letter from Mary Ann to her father had failed (the only letter she wrote him known to have survived), and when Mary Ann was talking wildly of going off to Leamington and teaching, he invited her to stay for a while at Griff. There, instead of reproaches, she received kindness and apparent understanding; and was brought round to agree to the outward compliance of church attendance, which was all her father required. Nine weeks after the storm broke, Mary Ann accompanied her father to church again, and did so for the rest of his life.

Maria Lewis believed that Mary Ann's fall into infidelity had been 'due to the over excitement, fostered by the Methodist Franklins and the Aunt, leading to a reaction', Mary Sibree that it was 'partly the result of disgust at the

'Coventry—our first vision in 1833', Sara Hennell wrote on the back of this watercolour she painted.

low moral standards of "Christians"'. Mary Ann, who had characteristically re-read the Bible from beginning to end before making her decision, told a friend in later years that Sir Walter Scott had begun the change – 'he was healthy and historical; it would not fit on her creed'. Undoubtedly, Charles Hennell's *Inquiry* and acquaintance with Bray crystallized her conversion. It must have been of this period that, as she told a much later friend, Edith Simcox, 'when walking near Foleshill she paused to clasp her hands with a wild aspiration that she might live "to reconcile the philosophy of Locke and Kant"'.

She could not but fear that some friendly relationships would be affected by her changed views. Mrs Sibree, at least, kindly assured her that this would not be so and, after some hesitation, allowed her to give free German lessons to their Mary. Did they come to regret their tolerance? Their son John corresponded with Mary Ann for some years; her letter to him on the French Revolution of 1848 is profoundly interesting, with her delight that she had, after all, seen a 'really great movement' in her own day, but fearing that any 'revolutionary animus' among our own less-well-educated masses would be 'simply destructive – not constructive'. But when John decided that he could not after all take orders, and ended up as a schoolmaster in Stroud and translator of Hegel, had Mary Ann's leaven been working? And Mary, who was to marry John Cash of the wealthy ribbon-making family and, after 1856, to live at Rosehill, revealed after George Eliot's death that the German lessons had included not only Mary Ann's realistic imitations of local rustic speech, but also discussions of the right to free love where marriage was not possible.

In all but outward compliance, Mary Ann's rebellion had been successful. It gained her complete freedom of views, since no one wished to force her again to visible demonstration of them. Henceforward the Brays were her preferred Coventry friends. In the summer of 1842, Cara's sister, Sara Sophia Hennell, came to Rosehill. She was seven years older than Mary Ann and had worked as a governess, most recently in the Bonham-Carter family. Sara was a woman of considerable though undisciplined intelligence, increasingly given to metaphysical speculation. In 1842, her mind met Mary Ann's in passionate affinity, and for the next twelve years Sara was to be Mary Ann's closest woman friend. Mary Ann had outgrown Maria Lewis. Already in 1841 she had suggested that they drop the language of the flowers from their letters; Maria had been Veronica, Martha or 'Patty' Jackson, an old school-friend, Ivy, and Mary Ann the twining Clematis for 'Mental Beauty'. Now her fervour was turned to Sara, to whom letters were signed, for a time at least, 'your loving wife Mary Ann', or sometimes Pollian or Dr Pollian, nicknames given her in the Bray family, with inevitable little jokes on Apollyan. She was to sign herself Pollian to Sara long after the old friendship had dwindled to a single birthday letter a year.

Charles Bray described Mary Ann as she was then:

We had frequently long walks together and I consider her the most delightful companion I have ever known: she knew everything. She had little self-assertion. Her aim was always to show her friends off to best advantage – not herself. She

Sara Sophia Hennell (1812–99): a watercolour by her sister Cara, *c.* 1833. When Sara met Mary Ann Evans, she was working as governess to the Bonham-Carter children, cousins of Florence Nightingale.

would polish up their witticisms, and give *them* the full credit for them. But there were two sides; hers was the temperament of genius, which has always its sunny and shady sides. She was frequently very depressed – and often very provoking, as much as she could be agreeable – and we had violent quarrels; but the next day, or whenever we met, they were quite forgotten, and no allusion made to them. Of course we went over all subjects in heaven and earth. We agreed in opinion pretty well at that time, and I may claim to have laid down the base of that philosophy which she afterwards retained. [that is, that the more people dwell on an invisible world, the more they neglect earthly duties] George Eliot also held with me . . . that one of the greatest duties of life was unembittered resignation to the inevitable.'

Mary Ann had been curious about phrenology before she met Bray. To him it was and remained a true science. His mentor was George Combe of Edinburgh, and Mary Ann willingly cut off her hair yet again so that Combe might better observe her 'bumps'. In 1844 Bray had a phrenological cast made of her head; unfortunately, her husband destroyed it after her death. George Combe's analysis, as Bray recounted it, reported a nervous, lymphatic temperament, active without endurance, the intellect greatly predominating in her brain development, the Animal and Moral regions about equal. Then 'The social feelings were very active, particularly the adhesiveness. She was of a most affectionate disposition, always requiring some one to lean upon, preferring what has hitherto been called the stronger sex, to the other and more impressible. She was not fitted to stand alone.'

(*Left*) The frontispiece to Vol. I of the fifth edition of George Combe's *A System of Phrenology*, 1843; first published in 1819 as *Essays on Phrenology*.

(*Right*) Mary Ann Evans; a pencil drawing by Caroline Bray, *c.* 1842.

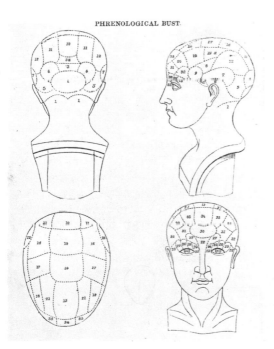

PHRENOLOGICAL BUST.

For several years she leant upon Charles Bray. Maria Lewis, visiting Rosehill, was shocked to see them walking arm in arm, 'like lovers' she said, and Sara Hennell confessed after Mary Ann's death that she had always disapproved of her 'depending so much on the arm of man'. But Cara Bray was not disturbed. An intelligent, self-contained woman, absorbed in her own work of writing educational books for schools, she retained Mary Ann's respect long after her feelings for Charles and Sara were no more than grateful if sometimes irksome remembrances. Moreover, Cara Bray probably had less reason for distress than some other women who were to be disturbed by Mary Ann's adhesiveness to their men. It was widely said that Cara's heart was given to Edward Noel, an illegitimate cousin of Lady Byron, who had given him an estate on the island of Euboea where he lived with his daughters for much of the year. According to Charles Hennell's wife, Bray 'promotes her [*sc.* Cara's] wish that Mr. Noel should visit Rosehill as much as possible and . . . she in return tries to promote his happiness in any way that his wishes tend'.

Charles Christian Hennell (1809–50); from a watercolour sketch by one of his sisters, probably Caroline, *c.* 1833.

Of the visitors to Rosehill, many were of a kind to interest and stimulate Mary Ann. George Combe who, phrenology apart, was an interesting and likable man, often came with his beautiful wife Cecilia, Sarah Siddons's daughter. Robert Owen came; he and Bray had much in common. There was young George Dawson, who was Carlyle's friend and a well-known lecturer; James Simpson, once a friend of Sir Walter Scott, an engaging anecdotist and advocate of free National Education; Dr John Conolly, devoted to the reform of lunatic asylums. Others, then less well known, would drop in. One was a young man called William Hepworth Dixon, who came to apply for the job of editing the *Coventry Herald* which Bray had bought in June 1846; Dixon's only credential was a manuscript tragedy, *The Azamoglan*, which he brought in his pocket, and he is the only person Bray writes unkindly of: '*We* thought him either too transcendant or too conceited for every-day work.' In later years Dixon became editor of the *Athenaeum*, and in 1859 wrote a cruel article on the author of *Adam Bede*; his reception at Rosehill may have rankled.

Cara's brother Charles Hennell came to Rosehill and perhaps briefly considered Mary Ann as a wife. But in 1842 there also came Elizabeth Rebecca Brabant, nicknamed Rufa for her red hair. Charles had asked to marry Rufa in 1839, but her father, Dr Robert Henry Brabant, had refused on grounds of Charles's poor health. But they still cared for each other, and there is no indication that this distressed Mary Ann. It was rather the family as a whole that she was then in love with.

Isaac could not continue to view these growing friendships with equanimity, and encouraged his father to protest. Mrs Pears tried to calm the old man down, and was told of Isaac's complaints that Mary Ann had no chance of getting 'a husband and a settlement, unless she mixes more in society . . . that Mr. Bray, being only a leader of mobs – can only introduce her to Chartists and Radicals, and that such only will ever fall in love with her if she does not belong to the Church.' Isaac was trying to persuade his father to move to Meriden where, surrounded by her family, Mary Ann might be brought to her senses.

But Robert Evans was now settled in Coventry society, and had no wish to leave. The new friendships could continue, Mr Evans even reconciling himself to doing without his daughter while she went travelling with the Brays, first to Malvern and Worcester in May 1843, then in July, on a tour through Bristol, Tenby, Pembroke and Swansea. They went to a public ball at Tenby, and poor Mary Ann had no partners; but Charles and Rufa, who had gone with the party, became engaged again. In late October, Mary Ann went with the Brays to London to be bridesmaid at Charles's and Rufa's wedding at the Unitarian Chapel in Finsbury on 7 November.

Rufa's father, Dr Brabant, had lost a daughter, but thought he might have found another. He was a German scholar – that is to say, he could read German and corresponded with David Friedrich Strauss – and was said to be collecting material for a major exegetic work which should finally dispose of the supernatural elements in Christianity; it never appeared. The Brays advised Mary Ann against accepting the Doctor's invitation to return to Devizes with him, but she, exalted by the prospect of attachment and service, would not listen. She was to be called Deutera, his second daughter, Dr Brabant told her, and on arrival at his home she flung herself at his feet, vowing devotion to his service. 'I am in a little heaven, here Dr. Brabant being its archangel', she wrote to Cara Bray.

But at the home in Devizes there also dwelt Dr Brabant's blind wife and his sister-in-law, Miss Susan Hughes, and they do not seem to have been unused to such situations. Mary Ann had passed only two weeks of an intended six weeks' stay when Miss Hughes began looking up trains and advising on routes back to Coventry. Dr Brabant cowered; even Rufa, who paid a visit on her return from her wedding journey, said that he acted 'ungenerously and worse towards Miss E', and it was a saddened and humiliated Miss E. who returned to Coventry after only four weeks.

Perhaps not unconnected with this unhappy visit was a fantasy which she wrote to a friend in 1846. She had dreamt, she said, of a dryasdust German professor who came to England in search of a wife; she must be ugly, a competent translator, and possessed of a little capital, and the professor found his ideal in Coventry in Mary Ann Evans. But before this wry fantasy was written, Mary Ann had had the chance, which was not to recur for many years, of a husband of her own who belonged to no one else. In the spring of 1845, when with the Houghtons at Baginton, she met a young painter and picture-restorer who was 'desperately smitten' and asked for her hand. 'We liked his letters to her very much   simple, earnest, unstudied', Cara Bray wrote to Sara.

Mary Ann, though not in love, decided she might become so, then decided she could not, and broke off the affair, clumsily and unkindly. 'My unfortunate "affaire" did not become one "du cœur",' she wrote to Sara, 'but it has been anything but a comfortable one for my conscience.' To Sara, her 'cara sposa', she represented it as an infidelity which, once over, left her again Sara's 'true Gemahlinn', this letter was signed 'your loving wife'. It would be incorrect to infer that Mary Ann had any homosexual leanings; but she needed, at all times, to be closest to *someone*, in a relationship of love.

'I am glad to hear that you approved dear Mrs. Bray's picture. I should think it is like, only that her benevolence extends to the hiding of faults in my visage as well as my character', Mary Ann wrote to Sara (16 September 1842) on the watercolour portrait above, which shows her with fair hair and blue eyes. Cara Bray had herself written sadly to Sara that 'I have been painting her the last fortnight, but I do not seem to improve.'

'We have seen more of M.A. than usual this week. She said she was Strauss-sick – it made her ill dissecting the beautiful story of the crucifixion, and only the sight of her Christ-image and picture made her endure it' – Cara to Sara, 14 February 1846. The 'Christ-image' (*above*) was a twenty-inch-high cast of Thorvaldsen's image of the risen Christ which Mary Ann kept in her study at Foleshill, and the engraving of Christ (*right*) she had considered using as a frontispiece to her translation; it was later given to John Sibree, and the statuette to Mrs Bray.

But now, as ever afterwards, there was work as recourse in distress. Charles Bray's *Coventry Herald* was open to her, and several pieces there have been identified as from her pen, including reviews of books on Christianity and other subjects, and five essays under the general heading 'Poetry and Prose from the Notebook of an Eccentric'. Four of them are worthily dull, anticipating the *Impressions of Theophrastus Such*; the fifth is a rather nauseating fantasy – 'Whenever a little acorn, or a beech nut, or any other seed of a forest tree begins to sprout, a little hamadryad is born, and grows up and lives and dies with the tree.' In September 1846 Sara Hennel wrote to her mother, 'M.A. looks very brilliant just now – we fancy she must be writing her novel', and a week later Mary Ann wrote to Sara, 'All the world is bathed in glory and beauty to me now.' But we know nothing more of this putative novel, or the reasons for this unusual happiness in a young woman too easily subject to depression and hysterical floods of tears.

It was not, however, as essayist or novelist that Mary Ann was to open her professional career, but as translator. The centre of the new explorations in religion, so absorbing to this group of friends, was Germany, and the great name there was that of David Friedrich Strauss, who had, incidentally, translated Charles Hennell's *Inquiry* into German. A group of Englishmen led by Joseph Parkes, the radical politician, decided to put up the money for an English translation of Strauss's *Das Leben Jesu*, published in 1843. Charles Hennell, entrusted with the task of finding the translator, first offered it to Sara, who declared it too difficult for her. Next he gave it to Rufa Brabant, who began the work but after her marriage did not want to continue. Early in 1844 Hennell offered it to Mary Ann.

Mary Ann had already some experience in translation. In 1842 she had made some translations from the Swiss Protestant theologian, Vinet, and the French Protestant historian, Guizot, at the suggestion of Francis Watts, and in 1843 from Spinoza's Latin for Cara Bray. She gladly accepted this new work and, with constant help from Sara, pursued it diligently. By the time the translation was completed, however, the original sponsors had lost interest, and only the energy of Charles Hennell and the private generosity of Joseph Parkes made publication possible. *The Life of Jesus Critically Examined by Dr. David Friedrich Strauss* in three volumes, the translator's name not given, was published on 15 June 1846 by Chapman Brothers of 121 Newgate Street, London, and for her labour Mary Ann received £20.

The Life of Jesus made no great stir, but it was recognized as a good translation and a sufficient passport to the working literary world that Mary Ann hoped to enter. But she was still in duty bound to her father and to the lives of her immediate family. Chrissey lost her little son Leonard in 1848 and Mary Ann, of course, went to Meriden, and there were visits to and from Fanny. Mary Ann was able to go on some trips with the Brays, in the summer of 1844 to the Lakes and again the next spring; and that autumn on an extended tour of Scotland. But increasingly her father needed her with him. She took him away for his health, to Dover in 1846, to the Isle of Wight in autumn 1847, and the next summer to St Leonard's; but he was clearly breaking up. It was a hard time for Mary Ann at home. Some of it she tried to fill by beginning a translation, which John Chapman had agreed to publish, of Spinoza's *Tractatus Theologico-Politicus*; and for consolation she, like Maggie Tulliver, read constantly in Thomas à Kempis's *De Imitatione Christi*, a book that was to be lying by her bed, with her Bible, when she died.

Mary Ann Evans, *c.* 1846, drawn by Sara Hennell from the shadow of a phrenological cast, presumably the cast of her head taken by James Deville of the Strand, London, in July 1844, at Charles Bray's instigation.

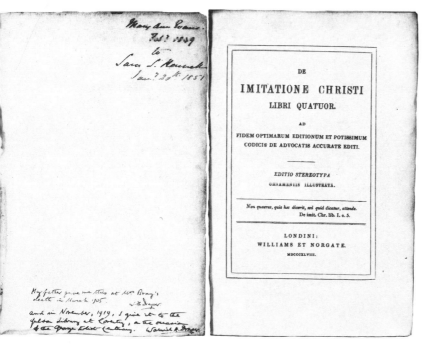

'I have at last the most delightful "de imitatione Christi" with quaint woodcuts. One breathes a cool air as of cloisters in the book' – Mary Ann to Sara, 9 February 1849. In 1851, she gave this copy to Sara.

But through Rosehill Mary Ann still retained contact with a wider world. Silly Dr Brabant hadn't given up hope. He was to be on the fringes of Mary Ann's circle for many years yet, but by 1846 she was able to write to Sara that 'I looked on my renewal of a correspondence with him as a favour *conferred* by me rather than *received*.' In July 1848, Ralph Waldo Emerson came to Rosehill. He was on a lecture tour of England and Bray had met him in London at the boarding-house run by John Chapman, his and Mary Ann's publisher. Mary Ann met Emerson at breakfast – 'the first *man* I have ever seen', she wrote to Sara – and straightway fell into earnest conversation with him. The watching Brays saw him start with surprise when Mary Ann, asked what book had first 'awakened her to deep reflection', answered, as Carlyle had done, Rousseau's *Confessions* (had she known these were started at Wootton Hall?). 'That young lady has a calm, serious soul,' Emerson said to the Brays.

The next year, 1849, on 30 May, Robert Evans died. 'What shall I be without my Father?' wrote Mary Ann as he lay dying. 'It will seem as if a part of my moral nature were gone. I had a horrid vision of myself last night becoming earthly sensual and devilish for want of that purifying restraining influence.'

Robert Evans had said to Isaac, shortly before his death, that he had left only a moderate estate from circumstances in which many men would have grown rich; 'but that he had always made it his first aim in life to do the best he could for all the clients who had employed him'. Still, he left what could fairly be called a tidy sum, and one that must have been almost entirely due to his private exertions. The size of his salary from the Newdigates is not known, but in the same district at the beginning of the century Lord Aylesford was giving his own land-agent £100 per annum. The farm at Kirk Hallam, now rented by the younger Thomas Evans, Robert Evans left to his elder son together with some property at Roston near Norbury. His Warwickshire

Robert Evans's tomb in Chilvers Coton churchyard; his funeral was on 6 June 1849. In this table tomb are also buried his second wife Christiana, and the short-lived twin sons, William and Thomas.

properties he left to Isaac. Fanny and Chrissey, who had each had £1,000 when she married, now received a further £1,000; Fanny got the Scott novels and the silver forks, Chrissey the silver spoons. Mary Ann was left the household effects (by a codicil, at the suggestion of Mr Vincent Holbeche, the lawyer, she received £100 in lieu) and £2,000 in trust, of which she could receive only the income. The five children shared equally in the residuary estate, the daughters' shares being on trust.

Under the will of Aunt Evarard of Attleborough, who had died, widowed, in 1844, Mary Ann received in trust, an eighth share of an estate valued at under £3,000, this, presumably, the little bit of capital referred to in her fantasy. (She also received, from among the meticulously listed possessions, 'my Watch, Twelve Tea Spoons and Sugar Bows [=tongs] and Four Salt Spoons marked M.P., my moreen Bed, Wardrobe and Chest of Drawers in my Bed Room, and the Clock in the Kitchen.') Thus Mary Ann had in all, so far as we know, a safe annual income of about £120, and whatever may have been her share in her father's residuary estate.

Within five days of the funeral the Brays took Mary Ann away for a tour of the Continent. They had hoped for the company of James Anthony Froude, who that year had published a heterodox novel, *The Nemesis of Faith*. Mary Ann had reviewed it in the *Coventry Herald* in March, and Froude, recognizing the style, had addressed a grateful note to 'The Translator of Strauss'. In June she had met Froude in London, and he had agreed to join the party; but instead of Froude there came a note to the station, saying that he was going to be married.

The Brays, with Mary Ann, took the traditional English travellers' route, to Paris, to Lyons, by boat to Avignon, to Marseilles, and along the coast road to Genoa. Though Mary Ann was still sadly distressed by the loss of her father, and, as always when distressed, in poor health, she acquired

Mrs John Evarard (*née* Mary Pearson) and a portion of her will. Aunt Evarard is recognizably the original of Aunt Glegg of *The Mill on the Floss*, who kept her best clothes unworn so that they could be admired after her death: 'Tom and Maggie considered their aunt Glegg as the type of ugliness....Mrs. Glegg had doubtless the glossiest and crispest brown curls in her drawers...but to look out on the week-day world from under a crisp and glossy front, would be to introduce a most dreamlike and unpleasant confusion between the sacred and the secular. Occasionally, indeed, Mrs. Glegg wore one of her third-best fronts on a week-day visit, but not at a sister's house...her long neck was protected by a *chevaux-de-frise* of miscellaneous frilling.' (Ch. VII.)

then a taste for foreign travel and especially for the sun and the south, and in later years, not only in happiness but equally in sick desperation, she would seek this panacea.

From Genoa to Como, then over the Simplon Pass to Martigny, the tour took the traditional route. The Simplon had to be crossed on mules, but Mary Ann bore the nerve-racking transit uncomplainingly, even though her side-saddle turned out to be ominously loose.

In Geneva the Brays left her. 'O the bliss of having a very high attic in a romantic continental town, such as Geneva,' she had written to young John Sibree a year earlier, and now, for ten months, she was to try it, at first in a *pension*, the Campagne Plongeon, just outside Geneva where the other guests included a Marquise who re-dressed Mary Ann's hair and abolished her abominable curls. As winter drew on, she moved into the city not to an attic but to a comfortable room in the *appartement* of Monsieur and Madame François D'Albert-Durade. Monsieur, only four feet tall, was a painter, Madame, whom Mary Ann soon called Maman, an excellent cook, and 'just the creature one loves to lean on and be petted by'. The D'Alberts were a cultured, musical family, and Mary Ann found their company and their circle congenial and soothing, though they were apt to be startled by Mary Ann's – or, as they called her, Minie's – still uncompromising religious views. D'Albert painted her portrait, and made a copy for her to take back to England. She worked for a time on the Spinoza translation, read, of course, voraciously, and attended lectures on experimental physics. It was with real regret that she left Geneva in March 1850. Monsieur D'Albert, though he could ill afford it, accompanied her to England; they crossed the Juras by sleigh through the still-deep snow. He stayed in London, to 'see the lions', as people still spoke of sightseeing. She went to Rosehill.

What was Mary Ann to do now? She went to stay with Isaac at Griff, and visited Fanny and Chrissey, but she knew that she did not want to live with her family. Monsieur D'Albert came to stay at Rosehill, and was taken on the local sightseeing round of Stratford and Kenilworth and Warwick Castle. We may wonder, with G. S. Haight, 'whether this was another case of Mary Ann's over-ready expansiveness betraying her into indiscretion', when we learn that D'Albert destroyed all the *tutoyer*-ing letters she wrote to him after he went home. Later he was to translate into French all George Eliot's novels (except *Felix Holt*) up to and including *Romola*.

Early that summer Mary Ann – or Marian, as she had now become, though she was trying out the name on the fly-leaves of her books by 1842 – had considered moving to London. She had written to Sara to ask the prices at the Chapmans' boarding-house at 142 Strand, on the site of the old Turk's Head Coffee House. Here, on the ground floor, John Chapman had his office and shop; above, the family lived and housed the boarders, some semi-permanent, others, like Emerson, visiting literary figures from abroad, for 142 Strand, despite Mrs Chapman's poor housekeeping, had a considerable reputation as a literary meeting-place.

John Chapman, then twenty-nine years old and dubbed, for his good looks, 'the Raffaele bookseller', was a Derby man; a large number of the

'For M. D'Albert I love him already as if he were father and brother both' (G.E. to the Brays, 24 October 1849). (*Above left*) Self-portrait of François D'Albert Durade (1804–86).

'I am sitting for my portrait – at M. D'Albert's request – not mine.' (G.E. to the Brays, 15 February 1850.) This is one of several copies, some made by D'Albert Durade himself, others after G.E.'s death.

The Campagne Plongeon, Lake Geneva, where Marian Evans boarded from late July till early October 1849.

John Chapman (1821–94) in later life. 'I did not know him till he was an old man, but even then he was beautiful', wrote T. P. O'Connor in 1899. O'Connor, walking down the Strand with Chapman, casually mentioned the rumour that 'before the days of George Henry Lewes, George Eliot had shown an inclination to adore another man.... Whereupon the still dandified octogenarian gave my arm an eloquent squeeze, and whispered, "You know she was very fond of me!" He said no more.'

people who became close to Marian came from her own parts of the country. He had married Susanna Brewitt from Nottingham, fourteen years older than himself but possessed of a little money. For all his professions – horologist in Australia, publisher and editor in London, and, finally, doctor practising in Paris – he was minimally qualified. He was also an inveterate amorist, and in 1850 the permanent residents of 142 Strand included not only himself and Susanna and their two young children, Beatrice and Ernest, but also his mistress, Elizabeth Tilley, loosely described as the children's governess, but in the census of 1851 simply as a visitor aged thirty.

Marian Evans had met John Chapman earlier, probably in 1846 when she went to London to stay with Sara, then living with her mother. 'I hope Mr Chapman will not misbehave, but he was always too much of the *interesting* gentleman to please me', she had written to Sara in 1847. Their first recorded meeting was at Rosehill in October 1850. Chapman had come with Robert William Mackay, whose *Progress of the Intellect* had just been published, to ask the translator of Strauss if she would write a notice of it, which the editor of the *Westminster Review* had agreed to take. This Marian did, and on 18 November took it to London and made a trial stay at 142 Strand. She enjoyed the literary Friday evenings, and enjoyed, too, meeting a young woman of twenty-eight, a former boarder there: probably a previous flame of Chapman's, certainly a one-time protégée of Dr Brabant's whom she had visited, after Marian, in 1847, before that the darling of old Walter Savage Landor, and, incidentally, the first woman to draw a regular newspaper salary. This was Eliza Lynn, who for many years after George Eliot's death was to be the only publicly hostile critic of George Eliot the woman. What she had to say is often dismissed as jealousy: her own novels had only a popular success, and her refusal to emigrate to America with her husband, James Linton, in 1867, was more lastingly strictured than Marian Evans's relationship with George Lewes came to be. But if George Eliot the woman is to be looked at with less than uncritical adulation, Eliza Lynn's comments must be considered, and often ring true.

On first meeting the two women apparently liked each other. Miss Evans reported that Miss Lynn had told her that 'she was never so attracted to a woman before as to me'. In her book *My Literary Life* of 1899, Mrs Lynn Linton recalled the meeting:

She was essentially under-bred and provincial; and I . . . was repelled by the unformed manner rather than attracted by the learning. She held her hands and arms kangaroo fashion; was badly dressed; had an unwashed, unbrushed, unkempt look altogether; and she assumed a tone of superiority over me which I was not then aware was warranted by her undoubted leadership.

'Then', Eliza, three years younger, had already published two novels, and Marian none; and Eliza was also prejudiced, she granted, by the fact that Marion had allowed the love-making of a certain unnamed man, which Eliza herself had found 'purely disgusting'. The following year Marian was called to add her weight to that of Chapman, Susanna and Elizabeth (the three women, as Kathleen Tillotson remarks, for once unanimous) in trying

Interior at Rosehill; Elizabeth Rebecca Hennell, *née* Brabant (1811–98), is on the left. Her nickname Rufa is said to have been given her by S. T. Coleridge.

to persuade Eliza to tone down some of the love scenes in her third novel *Realities*. They failed. Another publisher took the book, and Eliza's relationship to Marian remained that of desultory acquaintance in a common circle.

When Marian came back to Rosehill, her fortnight at the Chapmans', recounted as she sat 'in the red armchair with my feet in the fender', was deemed successful. She had attended lectures at the Ladies' College (later Bedford College), and among the people she had met at the Chapmans' soirées was 'good Mrs Hunt' – Mrs Thornton Hunt. After Christmas she returned to the Strand with the intention of boarding there, and, as a first piece of work, preparing an Analytical Catalogue of Chapman's publications. With Chapman's encouragement, she also proposed articles to both the *Edinburgh Review* and the *Westminster Review*; both refused her, but her article on W. R. Greg's *The Creed of Christendom*, intended for the latter paper, was accepted by Thornton Hunt for *The Leader* and appeared on 20 September 1851.

This second stay was unsuccessful in other than literary respects. A piano hired for Miss Evans at sixteen shillings a month had led to visits by Chapman to her room 'while she played one of Mosart's [*sic*] Masses with much expression', and a ganging-up between Susanna and Elizabeth resulted, as Chapman put it in his diary, 'in their comparing notes on the subject of my intimacy with Miss Evans and their arrival at the conclusion that we are completely in love with each other'. On 26 March, Chapman took Marian back to Euston Station where he had met her in January, assuring her, before 'the trains whirled her away very, very sad', that 'I felt great affection for her, but that I loved E. and S. also, though each in a different way.' At this avowal, Marian burst into tears.

But soon after her departure, Chapman had the chance of buying that eminent literary paper, the *Westminster Review*, which had been founded in

Kenilworth Castle, a favourite excursion from Coventry; a sketch made by Sara Hennell in 1836.

1824 by John Stuart Mill. With the help of backers, he succeeded in doing so for £300 – but who was to write its Introductory Prospectus? And who was to edit it? Chapman, of course, would be nominal editor, but he knew some of his limitations. It was essential to get Marian back.

There ensued months of painful negotiations, with three difficult women to be placated. Marian yielded at Kenilworth Castle where Chapman tactlessly discoursed 'on the incomprehensible mystery and witchery of beauty. My words jarred upon her and put an end to her enjoyment. Was it from a consciousness of her own want of beauty? She wept bitterly.'

Still, Marian had agreed to write the Prospectus and to come back to London, and eventually Susanna and Elizabeth agreed to her doing so. The domestic ménage, though henceforth calm, was never to be a happy one. With Chapman admitting 'beneficent affection . . . equally distributed towards Susanna, E. and M.', how could it be? It was not only the small close room, the London fogs, and the constant overwork that made Marian's stay in the Strand, from September 1851 to October 1853, a period of ill-health and recurrent spasms of black depression. 'Do write to me, dear Cara – I want comforting', she wrote typically in February 1852, ' – this world looks ugly just now.'

The work she had been brought there to do was superbly done. Tactfully Marian persuaded Chapman that his dignity as editor would be better sustained if he did not write for the paper; a later letter (25 June 1855), uncompromisingly tearing his style to pieces, confirms her judgment. Seldom if ever can a literary journal have had so competent an assistant editor as the *Westminster* in Marian Evans. There is a letter of hers to Chapman, written while on holiday in Broadstairs (July 1852), which is admirable in its sure grasp of the needs and problems of the paper; the authors likely to accept (Froude, Martineau), the need for something on Lamarck ('what do you say to Lewes . . .?'), and on Pre-Raphaelitism and on 'Hereditary Transmission', the immediate lack of good books for review ('nothing coming out which would do as a peg for an article'), and in the middle, surely wasted on

Chapman, her own religious position '. . . the thought which is to mould the Future has for its root a belief in necessity . . . a nobler presentation of humanity has yet to be given in resignation to individual nothingness, than could ever be shown of a being who believes in the phantasmagoria of hope sustained by reason.'

For her editorial work Marian was paid nothing. The Chapmans may have given her free or reduced board and lodging, for their cheapest rate for a 'Second class Bed room' was £2 5s a week; some unknown 'pecuniary arrangements with Marian E.' had been discussed between Chapman and Bray. But whatever these were, Marian had to count pennies. Her sister Fanny made clothes for her, but even so she had to refuse personal invitations for lack of the correct apparel. Her literary earnings at this period were minuscule, and up to the spring of 1854, when she gave up the editorial work, only two pieces in the *Westminster* are surely hers: the review of Mackay's *The Progress of the Intellect* in January 1851 and of Carlyle's *Life of John Sterling* in the first number under her editorship, that of January 1852. From the spring of 1853 she was working at a translation of Ludwig von Feuerbach's *Das Wesen des Christenthums* and for this Chapman agreed to pay 2s a page, some £30 in all. The project was to arouse ill-feeling. 'I bitterly regret that I allowed myself to be associated with your Series', Marian wrote in December 1853, in one of those determinedly rude letters to which she sometimes gave vent, ending, 'I fear some of my words may be illegible, which will be a pity because of course you can't substitute any half as good.' The only excuse for Chapman's meanness is that his own financial affairs, together with those of the *Westminster*, were always in a mess.

Pay apart, the work was rewarding. So was the social life, though often a strain that brought 'headaches and hysterics' in its train. Chapman had a knack of gathering congenial company at his evenings, now on Mondays, and, especially in 1851, the year of the Great Exhibition, innumerable visitors came: European writers and refugees like Karl Marx, Louis Blanc, Mazzini: from America, Horace Greeley, William Cullen Bryant, Noah Porter, later President of Yale, who found Miss Evans 'free and affable', but obviously preoccupied with her own world of 'elevated thoughts and intense feeling'. Among English visitors Marian met again George Combe and also Harriet Martineau whose acquaintance she had first made in Warwickshire in 1845. In October 1852 she managed a trip to the Combes in Edinburgh, staying with eccentric changeable Miss Martineau at Ambleside on the way back. Old Henry Crabbe Robinson came to the Chapmans, and, in 1852, Florence Nightingale, just back from Kaiserswerth and already a figure worth mentioning to Charles Bray, with the assurance that he would be pleased at Miss Nightingale's interest in his *Philosophy of Necessity*. Joseph Parkes came, who had paid for the Strauss translation, and with him his daughter Bessie, ten years younger than Marian, with a Warwickshire childhood and for many years to be Marian's friend, though that friendship was somewhat weakened by Bessie's increasing attraction to Catholicism and, in 1867, her French marriage to Louis Belloc (Hilaire Belloc was her son). Bessie had at first doubted whether Marian had any high moral purpose, but

Shortly after meeting Marian Evans, Bessie Parkes, then in her early twenties, wrote to Barbara Leigh-Smith: 'I don't know whether you will like Miss Evans. At least I know you will *like* her for her large unprejudiced mind, her complete superiority to most women. But whether you or I should ever *love* her, as a friend, I don't know at all. There is as yet no high moral purpose in the impression she makes. . . . I think she will alter.' (6 March 1852.)

Portrait of Herbert Spencer at the age of thirty-eight: 'My brightest spot next to my love of *old* friends, is the deliciously calm *new* friendship that Herbert Spencer gives me. We see each other every day and have a delightful *camaraderie* in everything.' (G.E. to Cara Bray, 27 May 1852.)

was soon writing to Barbara Leigh-Smith, who was to succeed Sara Hennell as Marian's closest and most nearly equal woman friend, that on better acquaintance she found that the 'harsh heavy look' of Marian's face 'softens into a very beautiful tender expression'. 'The odd mixture of truth and fondness in Marian is so great', she wrote to Barbara in 1853. 'She never spares, but expresses every opinion, good and bad, with the most unflinching plainness, and yet she seems able to see faults without losing tenderness.'

The first important man friend Marian made at 142 Strand was Herbert Spencer. Spencer, a Derbyshire man and a year younger than Marian, had been a civil engineer on the railways, sub-editor of the *Economist* since 1848, supporter of Chartism and Abolition: in 1851 his *Social Statics* had just been published. He and Marian became close friends, walking together in the Embankment Gardens to which Chapman had a key, visiting Kew – 'on a scientific expedition with Herbert Spencer, who has all sorts of theories about plants . . . if the flowers didn't correspond to the theories, we said *"tant pis pour les fleurs"*'.' Spencer, who was one of the people who suggested to Marian that she might write novels, took her to theatres and operas, and they had discreet holidays together at Broadstairs. Small wonder that, as Marian put it, 'all the world is setting us down as engaged.'

But Spencer, though he regarded Marian as 'the most admirable woman, mentally, I ever met', did not want to marry her, and did not scruple to tell her that her lack of beauty deterred him. She herself was always aware of this, writing sadly to the Brays of 'people who are short-sighted enough to like me'. But in Spencer's case we may suspect an excuse similar to Ruskin's when he told his bride Effie that it was distaste for her person that prevented his consummating their marriage, for Spencer remained a bachelor and slowly sank into self-obsessed valetudinarianism. Still, he kept a photograph of Marian in his bedroom until he died in 1903, admitting, when his sisters teased him, that he had been in love with her but that her long nose had made her difficult to kiss.

'We have agreed that we are not in love with each other,' Marian wrote of Spencer to the Brays in 1852, and the admission was probably the less painful in that Spencer's friend Lewes had entered her life as something more than a possible contributor to the *Westminster*.

George Henry Lewes, like Marian distantly of Welsh origin, was born in 1817, the son of John Lee Lewes, an actor and occasional writer. George had had a desultory education, and by 1852, having tried law, business, medicine and the stage, was in the literary world. He had published two novels and was now writing theatre notes and reviews of literature, especially German literature, and articles, ever-increasingly, on philosophy and science. He was to become the foremost scientific and philosophical popularizer of his time; his *Biographical History of Philosophy* of 1845–46, which he constantly revised, was used by university students well into this century, and I. P. Pavlov is one of many scientists whose special interest was first aroused by Lewes's *The Physiology of Common Life* of 1859–60. Lewes was not least concerned with attacking pseudo-science: spontaneous combustion as used by Dickens in *Bleak House*, spirit-rapping, clairvoyance and phrenology, over

which he crossed swords with Charles Bray in the *Leader* in 1853–54. Lewes's friend, the writer William Bell Scott was to write after his death: 'He ... never ceased to advance. At first he was only the clever fellow, but at a very early time he became the literary adept, then the able investigator, and lastly the scientific thinker and philosopher, one of the most trenchant and advanced minds in the science of this country.'

In 1841 Lewes had married Agnes Jervis, then aged nineteen: he was probably a tutor in her family. In addition to having a little money, which Lewes had not, Agnes was beautiful – he called her his Rose – and intelligent, supplementing the family income by translating French and Spanish. Until 1849 they were blissfully happy – 'a perfect pair of lovebirds', said Mrs Thomas Carlyle.

Lewes believed, with his friend Thornton Hunt (son of Leigh Hunt), that love must be free and untrammelled. 'George Lewes and Thornton Hunt were essentially free-thinkers', wrote Eliza Lynn Linton in 1899: 'Love alone was the sole priest needed – confession and inclination made the one binding tie and ceremony. Legal obligation was to them the remnant of a foregone barbarism, and enforced permanency was unholy tyranny.'

They lived as they believed. Thornton Hunt dwelt in a ménage known as 'the family Philanstery', first in Queen's Road, Bayswater, later in Hammersmith, with his wife, his wife's cousin and her husband, Samuel Laurence, the painter, the Egyptologist George Gliddon, and a couple of Hunt sisters. Not only the housekeeping was shared; and among the most frequent visitors were 'George Lewes and his pretty little wife Agnes'.

The Royal Botanic Gardens at Kew which Marian Evans visited with Herbert Spencer on what she called 'a *proof*-hunting expedition'. (G.E. to Sara Hennell, 29 June 1852.)

41

George Henry Lewes aged twenty-three, from a watercolour sketch by Anne Gliddon. '– the most amusing little fellow in the whole world – if you only overlook his unparalleled *impudence*, which is not impudence at all but man-of-genius *bonhomie*–' (Mrs Carlyle, *Letters*, 5 February 1849).

George and Agnes Lewes had four sons, Charles Lee, Thornton, Herbert and St Vincent, born respectively in 1842, 1844, 1846 and 1848. In 1850 St Vincent died, a week before Lewes and Hunt published the first number of their radical literary journal, *The Leader*. Two weeks later Agnes bore a fifth son, Edmund, whose father was Thornton Hunt. Lewes registered Edmund as his own child, but by October 1851, when Agnes bore Thornton's daughter, Rose, Lewes had ceased to regard her as his wife. It was in that month that he first met Marian Evans in a bookshop: 'a sort of miniature Mirabeau', she said.

Opinions on Lewes's appearance varied. Charlotte Brontë told Ellen Nussey that his face moved her almost to tears – 'it is so wonderfully like Emily'. Eliza Lynn Linton described him as 'a singularly plain man, deeply pitted with the smallpox, with narrow jaws and somewhat drawn-in cheeks. He had bright, vivacious, and well-shaped eyes, a quantity of light brown hair, and a flexible mouth of singular moistness.' Carlyle nicknamed him 'the Ape'. Douglas Jerrold said he was the ugliest man in London.

W. M. Thackeray's drawing of Agnes Lewes at the piano, with her husband beside her and Thornton Leigh Hunt looking on.

His amorous proclivities were well known. 'Frankly sensual, frankly self-indulgent', said Eliza, and disgusting even to men in his after-dinner conversation, but, she granted, 'wherever he went, there was always a patch of intellectual sunshine in the room.'

But when Lewes met Marian, he was run-down and depressed. At first he would call on her with Spencer, until there came an afternoon when Spencer took his leave, and Lewes stayed. In October 1853 Marian left the Strand for 21 Cambridge Street, Hyde Park Square, dingy lodgings brightened only by Barbara Leigh-Smith's loan of her own paintings. There, so Oscar Browning, a later friend and biographer of George Eliot, believed, their sexual relationship began.

On 20 July 1854, Lewes and Marian left England together. After a meeting at Cologne with Strauss, arranged by Dr Brabant whom they ran into on the way, they settled in the little principality of Weimar.

According to Marian, before they left England they told only two people, Bray and Chapman. But from the time she met Lewes, it is unwise to rely

43

on Marian's unsupported word in anything that concerned herself. Henceforward she would readily lie to save her convenience or her reputation. Thus we cannot know if the several people who claimed afterwards to have known were telling the truth. Mrs Belloc Lowndes, Bessie Parkes's daughter, asserts that Marian told Barbara and Bessie.

She asked my mother to walk round Hyde Park with her, and in the course of that walk she told her what she meant to do. My mother reminded her that she, Marian, had not liked Lewes at all when she first met him, and she told her the infinitely more serious fact that Mrs Gaskell knew a girl whom he had seduced, but that made no difference. She had quite made up her mind.

Nor can we be sure whether the departure was intended to inaugurate a permanent relationship. It has always been so understood, but a letter of Marian's to Charlie Bray, written from Weimar in October 1854, must raise doubts. In it she says, 'Circumstances, with which I am not concerned, and which have arisen since he left England, have led him to determine on a separation from Mrs. Lewes.' However this may be, the decision for permanency must have been taken by late August when Arthur Helps, Lewes's close friend, passed through Weimar and advised Marian to call herself Mrs Lewes, as, thereafter, she did. There could be no question of a divorce. Under the law as it then stood, Lewes, having once condoned his wife's infidelity, could not sue; and even after 1857, when the law was changed, this bar remained absolute.

To such a story there are always two sides, but Agnes's has gone by default. She has only two witnesses, neither provenly reliable. One was Eliza, who always defended Thornton Hunt as the scapegoat. In a letter to Spencer after Marian's death, she granted that Thornton was wrong to break the promise by which the connection was allowed by Lewes (perhaps that no children should be born of it?), but maintains that Thornton, 'so true to himself, so utterly apart from all time-serving, all worldliness', went to the wall, while Lewes and Marian, in their 'humbug and pastiche', received 'the reverence of the world'. The other witness is Halcott Glover, an American connection of Hunt's, who knew Agnes when young, and claims to have heard her story at second-hand from his aunt. As he told it in two romans à clef (Both Sides of the Blanket, 1945, and Louise in London, 1947), Lewes, with an illegitimate child of his own, encouraged Agnes's liaison with Hunt; Marian's visit to Agnes before the elopement, said on the one side to be to discover if Agnes would be hurt by it, was in fact to threaten Hunt's exposure and ruin if Agnes did not accept the situation unprotestingly; the later gossip presenting Agnes as having taken to drink was put about by Marian. The first and last of these accusations Glover repeated in a private letter to his friend Harold Rubinstein, and they may not be wholly untrue. When she felt herself threatened, Marian could react brutally, and when excited she could talk foolishly. In several letters she begs correspondents to forget indiscreet things she had just said to them, and in one to Bray (24 June 1859), she regrets cruel things said of Agnes. But whatever the truth may be, one version only has been accepted. Agnes, who had

44

two children by Thornton Hunt before he left her in 1858, sat alone on Campden Hill, and Marian, in the end, received the reverence of the world.

But in the summer of 1854, while George worked on his life of Goethe
and Marian wrote articles for the *Westminster* and for *Fraser's Magazine*
('Three Months in Weimar' was published there in 1855), literary London
was far from willing to accept the situation at the Leweses' valuation. In
Weimar, Marian was soon accepted: 'People are wonderfully kind to us
here', she wrote to Chapman, 'Liszt overwhelming in attentions.' London
would not follow suit. Carlyle, despite a long self-exculpatory letter from
Lewes, was contemptuous. Harriet Martineau convened a private meeting
of women to discuss the matter; 'Many present were very severe,' wrote
Arthur Paterson, whose mother had been there. An example of the extreme
reaction provoked is found in a letter from the sculptor Thomas Woolner to
William Bell Scott:

Have you heard of two blackguard literary fellows, Lewes and Thornton Hunt?
They seem to have used wives on the ancient Briton principle of having them in
common: now blackguard Lewes has bolted with a — and is living in Germany
with her . . . I will not any further lift the mantle and display the filthy contamina-
tions of these hideous satyrs and smirking moralists . . . stink pots of humanity.

Woolner's first reaction was by no means uncommon. Nor was his later one.
He was to become a frequent visitor to the Leweses.

Weimar as it was when Marian
Evans and George Lewes stayed
there, from 2 August to 3 November
1854–'a huge village rather than a
town,' she wrote to Charles Bray on
16 August, and 'I have had a month
of exquisite enjoyment, and seem to
have begun life afresh.'

45

Malvern, where Lewes often resorted to seek health, whether by means of Dr John Bilbirnie's Water Cure, described by 'Vivian' in the *Leader* (8 July 1854) as 'hydropathic salvation', or by Dr James Gully's 'cold packings' and sitz baths.

Why did the 'dear little man', as Marian often referred to Lewes, gain her lasting esteem? Undoubtedly there was strong sexual attraction; their friend Frederic Harrison's belief that the relationship was unconsummated in no way rings true. There was the urge to service which had imbued Marian's early relationships with men: Lewes's health was delicate, and in the spring of 1854, while he went to Malvern for a cure, Marian had been able to write some of his pieces for the *Westminster* and the *Leader* – though not his witty dramatic criticism under his gay-dog pseudonymous *persona* 'Vivian'. They had much in common, not only intellectual and artistic interests, but also a common streak of moral coarseness, of emotional vulgarity, already apparent in George and increasingly so in Marian. Then there was the influence of Feuerbach (*The Essence of Christianity* appeared under her own name Marian Evans, her only book to do so, in July 1854): Feuerbach held that, in the absence of God, the dominating motive of human relationships must be love. This would chime with Marian's long-held belief that love was justified where marriage was impossible; in 1848 she had written to Bray of *Jane Eyre*, 'All self-sacrifice is good – but one would like it to be in a somewhat nobler cause than that of a diabolical law which chains a man soul and body to a putrefying carcase.' Finally, there was the offer, at last, of 'some one to lean upon'.

Whether the relationship was one of absolute fidelity we do not know. 'I can only pray, against hope, that he may prove constant to her,' Chapman wrote to a friend, and doubts are inseparable from the conjunction of a notorious lecher with an ugly woman. During 1859–60 both were clearly in a poor nervous and moral state, and in December 1859 Marian wrote a

Daguerreotypes of Sara Hennell and Cara Bray, *c.* 1850.

description of Lewes to the D'Alberts: 'He is a person of the readiest, most facile intercourse – thoroughly acquainted with French literature – and of the most varied tastes. . . . He is a very airy, bright, versatile creature – not at all a formidable personage.'

Marian never used words carelessly, and, as compared with other enthusiastic portraits she wrote of Lewes, this one is suspiciously trivial. Her own fidelity is not in doubt. And whatever difficulties they may have had to work through before they attained lifelong devotion, a letter written by Marian to Cara in 1855 contained her enduring statement on the relationship as it existed during Lewes's lifetime:

. . . if there is any one action or relation of my life which is and always has been profoundly serious, it is my relation to Mr Lewes. . . . Light and easily broken ties are what I neither desire theoretically nor could live for practically. Women who are satisfied with such ties do *not* act as I have done – they obtain what they desire and are still invited to dinner.

Marian had left it to Bray to tell Cara and Sara. Cara wrote a letter of protest, then remained silent; though it was to her, in that family, that Marian's lasting admiration was given, her own fondness for Marian was always cooler than her husband's and sister's. Sara was distressed: 'I have a strange sort of feeling that I am writing to some one in a book, and not to the Marian that we have known and loved so many years. Do not mistake me, I mean nothing unkind', she wrote in November 1854, but with this shock, and with the Leweses' increasing impatience with Sara's mystical, undisciplined writing, that relationship withered.

Goethe's house in Weimar, which George Eliot described in her 'Three Months in Weimar' as 'much more important looking than Schiller's, but, to English eyes, far from being the palatial residence which might be expected, from the descriptions of German writers.'

At the beginning of November 1854 the Leweses moved to Berlin. Here Marian worked on her translation of Spinoza's *Ethics* (though completed, it has never been published), and helped Lewes by translating quotations for his book *The Life and Works of Goethe* which, when published the next year, immediately became the standard work. But despite a rewarding social life with Berlin's intellectuals, Marian found that winter cold and under-productive. In March 1855 they returned to England. Marian – or Polly, as Lewes called her – waited in Dover while Lewes went to London to look for lodgings and, it is said, to obtain assurance from Agnes that the break was final. In mid-April Marian came to London, to lodgings at 8 Victoria Grove Terrace (now Ossington Street) in Bayswater. Here Eliza Lynn Linton called – she says at the Leweses' request – and of this visit (which she wrongly places in St John's Wood) her account is so sympathetic as to be some validation of her other less kind perspectives:

. . . the aureole of their new love was around them [she writes]. There was none of the pretence of a sanctioned union which came afterwards. . . . She was frank, genial, natural, and brimful of happiness. The consciousness that she had finally made her choice and cast the die which determined her fate, gave her a nobility of

48

expression and a grandeur of bearing which she had not had when I first knew her. Then my heart warmed to her with mingled love and admiration. . . . I felt her superiority and acknowledged it with enthusiasm. Had she always remained on that level, she would have been the grandest woman of this or any age.

Their only other callers were Chapman, Rufa Hennell and Bessie Parkes, who for some time thereafter had to be reminded to ask for and address letters to 'Mrs Lewes'. By the beginning of May they had found lodgings at 7 Clarence Row, East Sheen, an area convenient for long walks, which they loved, in Kew Gardens and Richmond Park. But in early October, after Lewes had spent a week at Ramsgate with his three sons and then, with Marian, a fortnight at Worthing, they moved to better accommodation at 8 Park Shot, Richmond, where they were to stay for three years. They saw few people there. When Lewes was at home, they would spend the evenings reading to each other, or sometimes playing the piano and singing, though fearful of disturbing the clergyman in the rooms below. Once a week Lewes would go to London, to deliver their manuscripts, to see his mother, Mrs John Willim, and his sons who, officially at least, knew nothing of the new situation.

The Pariser Platz, Berlin. 'Berlin is a cold place. . . . We work hard in the mornings till our heads are hot, then walk out, dine at three and, if we don't go out, read diligently aloud in the evening. I think it is impossible for two human beings to be more happy in each other', Marian wrote to Charles Bray (12 November 1854).

A so-called 'Balloon Map' of London in 1851 as seen from Hampstead. In the foreground, from east to west (that is, left to right) are the districts of Marylebone, St John's Wood and Paddington, in which, at various times, George Eliot lived.

Fortunately, Marian now had work to do. Chapman had given her the editorship of the Belles Lettres section of the *Westminster* at twelve guineas a quarter, and in the issues dating from October 1854 ('Women in France', written in Weimar) to January 1857, the *Westminster*'s literary section was enriched by some fine articles from her pen – anonymous, as almost all reviewing was to be until the appearance of the *Fortnightly Review*, edited by Lewes, in 1865. *The Essays of George Eliot* edited by Thomas Pinney (1963) contains almost all her occasional work of this kind, which is remarkable for its stern thoughtfulness and profound erudition. Among the best may be noted 'Evangelical Teaching: Dr Cumming' (October 1855), a beautifully reasoned and uncompromising attack on a 'lax and slippery' popular cleric, and 'Silly Novels by Lady Novelists' (October 1856), especially interesting as giving Marian's views on fiction shortly before she was to begin her own.

But there was little money in this work, and the Leweses were poor. In 1855, for eight articles, Marian earned £119 8s. Lewes's annual earnings in this period ranged from something over £300 to about £600. He was legally responsible for supporting Agnes and not only his own sons but also her

objections I must suggest
that the phrase "Design of
Creation" is equivocal. It
may mean "the final cause
of the Universe as a whole"
& is more likely to suggest
that idea than what I
imagine you mean, namely,
the final causes of things
considered individually.

Herbert Spencer is coming
to dine with us tomorrow,
having come back from
Paris weary of solitary
sight-seeing.

Ever your affectional
Marian

children by Hunt; he allowed her some £250 a year, which had occasionally to be supplemented when she fell into debt.

Marian had not yet told her family of her new relationship. Lewes's Christmases were usually spent with the Helpses, and Marian spent the Christmas of 1855 with Chrissey. Chrissey's husband, Edward Clarke, had died in 1852, leaving Chrissey with only about £100 a year on which to bring up her family, and she was living rent-free in Aunt Evarard's former house in Attleborough, now owned by Isaac. Charles Bray suggested that Marian call at Rosehill on the way home, and her reply displays the touchiness that was, almost inevitably, to mar her in the coming years: 'If you had thought twice you would have seen that I was not likely to take a journey twice as long as necessary and walk all through Coventry in order to make a call where I had only the invitation of the master of the house.'

Still, such friends as she had made, and they were not yet many, stood by her as far as she would let them. Charles Bray had called at Richmond and so did Spencer and Chapman. The correspondence with Sara was resumed and, more haltingly, with Cara. Rufa Hennell would come (her husband had

Letter from Marian to Sara, written at Richmond on 8 November 1856, pointing out that the passage Sara had written on 'design' was self-contradictory: 'if you mean...that there is a Being who has the same relation to the eye as a piano maker has to a piano, why do you appear to range yourself with the antagonists of Natural Theology, since you admit its fundamental principle?...Apart from all these objections...' *etc.*

died in 1850, and in 1857 she was to marry Mark Call, a clergyman who had resigned his orders). Bessie Parkes came – 'Your address to me as *Miss Evans* was unfortunate' – and so did Barbara Leigh-Smith, though at present absorbed in her own extraordinary affairs. For in June 1854 the Chapmans had given up 142 Strand and moved to 43 Blandford Square, where neighbours at No. 5 were Barbara's father, the liberal-minded Benjamin Leigh-Smith, and his illegitimate but acknowledged family. Chapman and Barbara fell in love. He proposed they should live openly together. Onlookers hinted that the £300 a year with which Mr Smith had endowed each of his children was no small part of the inducement, but Chapman himself argued to Barbara that 'Lewes and M.E.' seemed to be perfectly happy – a useful example of an important reason why even sympathetic people felt they could not condone 'hard-case' examples of extra-marital relationships lest they act as trail-blazers; it was one of Marian's fears that her own action should be so used rather than regarded as exceptional. Barbara eventually told her father, who acted promptly. Barbara's brother, Ben, took her off to Algiers where she met the eccentric, romantic, generous Dr Eugène Bodichon, and married him in June 1857.

The year before, Barbara had joined the Leweses on a happy summer holiday at Tenby: it was there that Marian told Barbara that she and George had decided not to have children and were practising contraception; unfortunately, Mrs Belloc Lowndes destroyed the letter in which Barbara reported this to Bessie. The Leweses had gone to Tenby after a stay at Ilfracombe where George had initiated his Polly into the beauties of polyps and zoophytes, aided by a microscope lent by Arthur Helps; in 1858 Lewes was to publish *Sea-Side Studies*, 'the book of all my books', he wrote in 1876, 'which was to me the most unalloyed delight.'

Marian's obsessive insistence that her relationship with Lewes should be regarded as a marriage steadily grew, and with it her ever more marked and embarrassing references to him as 'my husband'. She became resolved that her own family should accept the situation. Relations with Isaac had been uneasy for years, and in 1852, when Marian went to Meriden to comfort Chrissey after her husband's death, Isaac had been furious with Marian for arranging to leave without consulting him, and told her she need never apply to him for help. But this was probably only family hot temper, for in the summer of 1855 Marian was able to tell Charles Bray that she had had a kind letter from her brother, and as late as April 1857 Marian and Isaac were in friendly correspondence over Chrissey's affairs. By this date Marian's family must have had some inkling of her private life and preferred to know nothing officially. Marian determined that they should. In May 1857 she wrote to Isaac to say that she had changed her name 'and have someone to take care of me in the world. . . . My husband has been known to me for several years, and I am well acquainted with his mind and character. He is occupied entirely with scientific and learned pursuits. . . .'

As Marian's trustee under their father's and Aunt Evarard's wills, it was not improper that Isaac should have instructed Vincent Holbeche, the family lawyer, to reply, asking for formal details of the marriage, though if Isaac

Dr Eugène Bodichon (1810–86), who practised medicine among the Arabs in Algiers and worked for the abolition of slavery. 'Dr. and Mrs. Bodichon came a few days after you left us. We think the *essential* is there – that he is a genuine, right-feeling man', G.E. wrote to Sara Hennell on 19 August 1857.

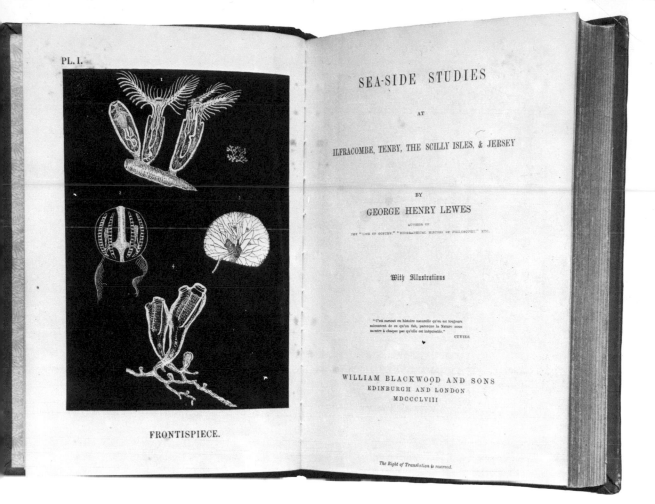

PL. I.

FRONTISPIECE.

SEA-SIDE STUDIES

AT

ILFRACOMBE, TENBY, THE SCILLY ISLES, & JERSEY

BY

GEORGE HENRY LEWES

AUTHOR OF
THE "LIFE OF GOETHE," "BIOGRAPHICAL HISTORY OF PHILOSOPHY," ETC.

With Illustrations

"C'est surtout en histoire naturelle qu'on est toujours
méconteut de ce qu'on fait, parcequc la Nature nous
montre à chaque pas qu'elle est inépuisable." — CUVIER.

WILLIAM BLACKWOOD AND SONS
EDINBURGH AND LONDON
MDCCCLVIII

The Right of Translation is reserved.

was ignorant of the real state of affairs, this was an unlikely first response. But on Marian's – no doubt expected – statement of the more exact facts of the situation, Isaac chose to break off all relations with his sister, and forced Chrissey and Fanny, who had already replied kindlily to similar if still more misleading letters from Marian, to do the same. He did not relent until his sister was a legally married woman.

Though Marian never ceased to feel bitter over her family's condemnation, other and substantial consolations were burgeoning. There had been talk of novel-writing at Foleshill, and later with Spencer. At some past time, perhaps at Foleshill, Marian had written the first chapter of a novel about rural life in Staffordshire, but had felt herself too 'deficient in dramatic power, both of construction and narrative', to go on. She 'happened' to have his fragment with her in Germany, and in Berlin, in the winter of 1854, she read it aloud to Lewes. He too, though struck with the fragment, doubted her capacity, but still thenceforward would say to her, very positively, 'You must try and write a story', and at Tenby, in the summer of 1856, was urging her to begin. She put it off, and then, as she described it:

In Lewes's *Sea-Side Studies*, he incorporated many of Marian's descriptions of the Ilfracombe scenery from her *Journals*, and added such sprightly 'expedition-sketches' of his own as 'My companion, whose legs are lolling in a shallow pool, brings out a pocket-pistol [*sc.* flask] of sherry and a bag of biscuits.

53

John Blackwood (1818–79), of the firm of William Blackwood and Sons, Edinburgh: 'My Dear Sir, Along with this I send a copy of the January number of the Magazine in which you will find the first part of Amos Barton.... It is a long time since I have read anything so fresh so humorous and so touching.' (Blackwood's first letter to G.E., 29 December 1856.)

. . . one morning as I was lying in bed, thinking what should be the subject of my first story, my thoughts merged themselves into a dreamy doze, and I imagined myself writing a story of which the title was – 'The Sad Fortunes of the Reverend Amos Burton'. I was soon wide awake again, and told G. He said, 'O what a capital title!' and from that time I had settled in my mind that this should be my first story.

They returned to Richmond on 9 August, and Marian was anxious to begin. First she had to finish two articles for the *Westminster*. Then, on 23 September, she wrote in her Journal, 'Begin to write "The Sad Fortunes of the Reverend Amos Burton", which I hope to make one of a series called "Scenes of Clerical Life".'

Through the autumn she wrote, though with diffidence and doubt when she had written. That she could manage dialogue Lewes soon granted, but pathos? Could she bring off Milly Barton's death? An evening came when Lewes went to town, leaving Marian alone to try, and when he came home, she read him what she had written. They cried together, and he kissed her and said, 'I think your pathos is better than your fun.'

Henceforward, for better and for worse but more often the former, Lewes was to be in effect Marian's literary agent, and nowhere did he serve her better than in choosing her publisher. John Blackwood of Edinburgh (1818–79), in addition to running the family publishing firm, had taken over the family publication *Blackwood's Magazine*, then and still known as *Maga*. Lewes had already published there; the magazine was currently running his 'Sea-Side Studies'. It was, then, to John Blackwood that Lewes sent the manuscript of 'Amos Barton' on 6 November 1856, as a story by a male friend.

'I am happy to say', Blackwood wrote to Lewes, 'that I think your friend's reminiscences of Clerical Life will do,' but cautiously he wanted to see more before giving a definite acceptance. But, on being told of the clerical friend's disappointment, Blackwood agreed to publish 'Amos Barton' without more ado, the first of two parts to appear in *Maga* in January 1857. 'I am glad to hear', he wrote, 'that your friend is as I supposed a Clergyman. Such a subject is best in clerical hands.' In explaining that he had used 'clerical' only loosely, Lewes warned Blackwood, as in years to come he was repeatedly to do, of his friend's 'shy, shrinking, ambitious nature' and his easily shaken confidence. In January 1857 Blackwood was happy to be able to tell the diffident author that he had shown the manuscript to Thackeray with the words, 'I have alighted upon a new Author who is uncommonly like a first class passenger,' and that Thackeray, glancing at it, had remarked that he would have liked to read more.

On Christmas Eve, 1856, Lewes had gone off to spend his usual couple of weeks with Arthur Helps, and that evening Marian began writing 'Mr Gilfil's Love Story'. On New Year's Day the first instalment of 'Amos Barton' appeared. On 4 February 1857 Marian told Blackwood, who had not yet been given the name of his new author, that a *nom de plume* had been decided on 'and accordingly I subscribe myself, best and most sympathizing of editors, Yours very truly, George Eliot.' (Many years later she told her husband that she had chosen George because it was Lewes's name, and Eliot for 'a good mouth-filling, easily-pronounced word'.) 'Mr Gilfil' was finished in the Leweses' spring holiday in the Scilly Isles, and appeared in *Maga* from March to June 1857. 'Janet's Repentance' was straightway begun, finished in Jersey on 30 May, and published from July to November. A fourth Scene, to be called 'The Clerical Tutor', had been projected, but it was not – or not then – written; an entry in Marian's Journal of 30 November 1858, on the genesis of *Adam Bede*, indicates that this too was originally intended to be one of the Scenes, but that 'several motives' had induced her to close the Scenes with 'Janet's Repentance'.

For the three stories in eleven instalments in *Maga*, Marian received £263, and for the book publication in two volumes, which appeared in January 1858, £180 on an edition of 1,000 copies at 21*s*. Nine presentation copies were sent out at the author's request; the recipients were Dickens, Thackeray, Tennyson, Ruskin, Faraday, J. A. Froude, Mrs Carlyle, Albert Smith (a popular lecturer and entertainer) and Arthur Helps.

In literary circles the book was well received. The few reviews – only three! – were encouraging. The presentees wrote graceful letters. Only Dickens guessed the author to be a woman. Himself the master of domestic detail, he inferred this from the 'womanly touches': 'all the references to children, and . . . such marvels of description as Mrs Barton sitting up in bed to mend the children's clothes'. Mrs Carlyle made a sprightly guess at 'a man of middle age, with a wife from whom he has got those beautiful *feminine* touches'. Many years later, Herbert Asquith, then an undergraduate at Balliol, asked George Lewes whether a reader should have been able to guess the writer's sex, and, if so, how. Lewes replied that he thought the best evidence was the virtual lack of reference to field-sports.

But if the mild stir the stories caused among literary people could be considered satisfactory and encouraging, in Warwickshire there was furore. The events of all three stories had their counterparts in reality. So did the places. So did almost all the characters. What George Eliot – all-importantly – fleshed in creative interpretation were the bones of stories of which the first and third, and substantially the second, corresponded to locally known facts. And in view of her later denials of identities, it is worth noting a letter to Blackwood of June 1857, before 'Janet's Repentance' was published, assuring him that her sketches both of clergymen and of dissenters, were 'drawn from close observation of them in real life, and not at all from hearsay or the descriptions of novelists'.

In 'real life' Amos Barton was John Gwyther, curate-in-charge of Chilvers Coton Parish Church from 1831 to 1841: Mary Ann Evans would have known him well, and witnessed his abrupt departure from the pulpit. His wife Emma, whose sad story was locally well known, is buried in Chilvers Coton churchyard. Her fictional name is that of a sister of Sir Roger Newdigate's second wife, the Newdigate name itself easily recognizable as 'Oldinport'. Sharp-tongued kindly Mrs Hackit was identified as Mrs Robert Evans, though Mrs Evans could not have attended the deathbed of 'Milly' who died after her, in November 1836.

(*Above*) Astley Castle, Arbury, home of Francis Newdigate II and his wife Lady Barbara; in *Mr Gilfil's Love-Story*, Knebley Abbey, home of Mr Oldinport and Lady Felicia.

(*Right*) Sir Roger Newdigate and his second wife Hester–Sir Christopher and Lady Cheverel of *Mr Gilfil's Love-Story*.

The events recounted in the third story, 'Janet's Repentance', took place in Nuneaton in 1829, when Mary Ann was at school there. Again, every place, every character, almost every episode had its real-life counterpart. Lawyer Dempster and his wife were Mr and Mrs Buchanan, she the daughter of Mrs Wallington whose school Mary Ann had attended, their house still standing in Church Street, the 'Orchard Street' of the story. The Reverend Mr Tryan was John Edmund Jones, whose Evangelical sermons had sparked off riots. In many of the fictional names George Eliot was, as in the first story, careless of concealment, the distinctively named Honourable and Reverend Mr Stopford becoming the fictional 'Honourable and Reverend Mr Prendergast', and Stockingford 'Paddiford'.

In 'Mr Gilfil's Love Story', which Queen Victoria liked the best of the three, Mr Gilfil was based on the Reverend Bernard Gilpin Ebdell, who, as Vicar of Chilvers Coton from 1786 until his death in 1828, had christened Mary Ann. Cheverel Manor is photographically Arbury Hall and the Cheverels are Sir Roger Newdigate and his second wife. 'Caterina' had her original in Sally Shilton, daughter of one of the local colliers, whom Lady Newdigate had heard singing on a cottage doorstep when still a child. She was taken to the Hall, trained by an imported Italian singing master and gradually treated by the childless Newdigates more and more as a daughter. But her health broke down, possibly, writes Lady Newdigate-Newdegate in *The Cheverels of Cheverel Manor* (1898), as the result of an unhappy love-affair, and in 1792–93 she was sent on a recuperative journey abroad. She married Mr Ebdell in 1801, but, unlike her fictional counterpart, had over twenty-three years of married life. Mary Ann would often have met her and her pretty daughter Anne, born in 1807, who married Latimer Harper, the brother of the 'secondary squire'.

'They laid her in the grave – the sweet mother with her baby in her arms.' In *Amos Barton* (Ch. IX) the grave of Milly in Shepperton churchyard, in fact the grave of Emma Gwyther at Chilvers Coton.

In fact, the home of Mr and Mrs Buchanan, in Church Street, Nuneaton; in *Janet's Repentance*, the home of Lawyer and Mrs Dempster in Orchard Street, Milby.

Is either of these men an original for Captain Wybrow? Charles Parker I (*above*), usually accepted as such, but a generation older than Sally Shilton, at the time of her putative love-affair a married man, and his son, after his own death in 1795, accepted as Sir Roger Newdigate's heir; or Francis Newdigate II (*opposite*), near Sally's age, an Army officer, and, though the son of the elder brother, cut out of the Arbury inheritance?

Captain Wybrow is usually identified with Charles Parker, Sir Roger's favourite nephew, who died a natural if premature death in 1795. This is accepted by Lady Newdigate-Newdegate, though she points out that Charles Parker was born in 1756, Sally Shilton in 1774, and that in 1785, when Charles married, Sally was only eleven. A more likely original is the somewhat shadowy Francis Newdigate II, Robert Evans's boyhood friend, who actually appears in the first chapter of the story as the unpopular Mr Oldinport. Francis Newdigate II was almost the same age as Sally Shilton. He was, like Captain Wybrow, an army officer. And he was, for reasons of which we know nothing, passed over in the inheritance save as an improbable last resort and otherwise omitted from Sir Roger's generous last will.

But whatever may be the validity of this last supposition, enough identifications were made for eager surmise in Warwickshire. Who could be the author? Such scenes as those at the Red Lion Inn made a woman unlikely, at least to those who had forgotten the likelihood of Robert Evans's bringing home stories from its original, the Bull Hotel in Nuneaton. It seems surprising that the Newdigates did not think of the young woman who had been given the run of the library, but apparently they did not. Isaac Evans, it was later said, knew immediately that his sister was the author, but held his tongue. Eventually local opinion settled on a Mr Joseph Liggins.

Liggins, whom Marian remembered from her childhood as 'a tall black coated genteel young clergyman-in-embryo', was the son of an Attleborough baker. He had been rusticated from Cambridge, and some time during the 1820s had lived in the Isle of Man. There the local newspaper, the *Manx Sun*, published a note on 4 July 1857, identifying 'Liggers', as they called him, as the author of the *Scenes*. The news quickly spread, and was reported by Fanny in a letter to Marian – this was just before Isaac forced the rupture of relations – who replied that she and Mr Lewes had been struck with the *Scenes* and had recognized 'some figures and traditions': but the author was a Mr Eliot, presumably a clergyman.

Not surprisingly, given the many correspondences with reality, other difficulties arose. Blackwood received a troubled letter from a Mr Jones who had recognized his brother in Mr Tryan. 'No portrait was intended', George Eliot wrote firmly: she knew only 'the *outline*' of the controversy she had depicted – 'The details have been filled in from my imagination.' Mr Gwyther, it turned out, was alive and living in Yorkshire. To his letter protesting his 'pained feelings at making public my private history', George Eliot could only reply that she was 'sincerely sorry' but she had thought he was dead: still, it was careless of her not to have checked in *Crockford*'s. His portrait was one of the only two she admitted to. The other was that of Lawyer Buchanan who, she wrote to Bray in September 1859, 'was by no means so witty, I imagine, as his representative in "Janet".'

By the time that Marian wrote this letter, *Adam Bede* had been published. She had started in October 1857. 'It will be a country story – full of the breath of cows and the scent of hay', she wrote to Blackwood. John Blackwood was already beginning to suspect the identity of his new author. His brother, Major William Blackwood, had called at Richmond in December 1857 to discuss a book of Lewes's, and wrote to Edinburgh that 'G.E. did not show: he is such a timid fellow, Lewes said . . . I saw *a* Mrs Lewes.' 'It was evident to us', Marian wrote in her Journal, 'that he knew I was George Eliot.' But it was not until February 1858 that the declaration was made in form. John Blackwood called at Richmond, and asked, 'Well, am I to see George Eliot this time?' 'Do you wish to see him?' Lewes asked. 'As he likes – I wish it to be quite spontaneous.' Marian left the room, then told Lewes, who had followed her, that he might reveal her. 'Blackwood was kind', she wrote. To his wife, Blackwood said, 'She is a most intelligent pleasant woman, with a face like a man, but a good expression', and he stressed the extreme desirability of not letting the secret out. He was afraid, and the Leweses terrified, that if George Eliot's identity became known, the then scandalous liaison would stop sales; indeed, Barbara Bodichon later reported a friend as saying that if the authorship of *Scenes* and *Adam Bede* had been known, every newspaper critic would have written against them.

It was decided that *Adam Bede* should be published straightway in book form, and not first serialized in *Maga*. Marian was working on it through most of 1858, through the three months spent in Munich from April to July (lodgings 10s a week, table d'hôte 1s 3d each), distracted, though pleasantly, by a tour to Salzburg, Vienna and Prague where they visited the old synagogue, and then to Dresden where they stayed till the end of August. Marian wrote her 'Jubilate' for the book's completion in her Journal on 16 November in London. Blackwood gave £800 for four years' copyright. The book was published on 1 February 1859. This time seven presentation copies were sent out, to Dickens, Thackeray, J.A. Froude, Charles Kingsley, Richard Owen, Dr John Brown, and Mrs Carlyle. After Lewes's death, Marian said that she had disliked this practice – 'It was always my husband who desired them to be sent.'

The success of *Adam Bede* was immediate, the reviews glowing. The anonymous reviewer in *The Times* (E.S. Dallas) wrote typically, 'It is a first-rate novel, and its author takes rank at once among masters of the art'; and he expressed the then general view when he said that the gem of the novel was Mrs Poyser. It was on Mrs Poyser that George Eliot's reputation with the general reading public was made. ('I like to trace a likeness to the dear Highlanders in Adam – & also in Lisbeth & Mrs Poyser', wrote Queen Victoria, who commissioned two paintings of favourite scenes from the novel.) For many years admiring comparisons were to be made with the faithful verisimilitude of Dutch paintings, and as each new novel appeared, library readers looked first to see if there was anything like Mrs Poyser in them. It was a long way from Anne Fremantle's interesting judgment in her *George Eliot* (1933) that *Adam Bede* is a cruel book, that Hetty, like other of George Eliot's heroines, suffered retributive justice for Marian Evans's sins.

But after the first delights of universal approbation, the publication of *Adam Bede* brought troubles which reduced the Leweses to a state of nervous, obsessive fractiousness from which they did not emerge for some time and not with much credit. Inevitably, rumour swelled around George Eliot's identity. Already in November 1858 Spencer, to whom alone the secret had

Dinah Morris preaching on Hayslope Green, commissioned by Queen Victoria from E. H. Corbould. 'Dinah walked as simply as if she were going to market, and seemed as unconscious of her outward appearance as a little boy: there was no blush, no tremulousness, which said, "I know you think me a pretty woman, too young to preach;"... It was one of those faces that made one think of white flowers with light touches of colour on their pure petals. The eyes had no peculiar beauty, beyond that of expression; they looked so simple, so candid, so gravely loving, that no accusing scowl, no light sneer could help melting away before their glance.' (*Adam Bede*, Ch. II.)

been confided a year earlier, told the Leweses that he had been asked point-blank by Chapman if George Eliot was Marian Lewes and, unable to tell a point-blank lie, had prevaricated. The Leweses were furious with Spencer for his mealymouthedness, and he was not forgiven for some months; he was jealous of 'our' success, Lewes wrote in his Journal. Marian repaid Chapman's surely excusable curiosity with one of her brutal letters, and in her Journal she wrote that she would not willingly correspond with or see him again. Lewes decided that their policy should be that of Sir Walter Scott in similar circumstances: that absolute denials should be made. 'I am of Scott's opinion on that point', Marian wrote to Blackwood, though in 1839, when

'There is one order of beauty which seems made to turn the heads not only of men, but of all intelligent mammals, even of women. It is a beauty like that of kittens, or very small downy ducks making gentle rippling noises with their soft bills, or babies just beginning to toddle and to engage in conscious mischief–a beauty with which you can never be angry, but that you feel ready to crush for inability to comprehend the state of mind into which it throws you. Hetty Sorrel's was that sort of beauty.' *Hetty and Captain Donni-thorne in Mrs Poyser's Dairy*, com-missioned by Queen Victoria from E.H. Corbould. (*Adam Bede*, Ch. VIII.)

she had read Lockhart's *Life of Scott* at Foleshill, her response had been, 'The spiritual sleep of that man was awful: he does not at least betray if he felt anything like a pang of conscience.' Consequently, when Chapman wrote again, he received a letter from Lewes stating that his continued imputation of the works to Mrs Lewes was an offence against delicacy and friendship – 'she authorizes me to state, as distinctly as language can do so, that she is not the author of "Adam Bede".' Marian's agreement to the policy of denial had, however, been reluctant; and in 1876, when discussing lying with Emily Davies, the educationalist, she maintained that she had not known of the denials Lewes had made on her behalf in 1859.

On 19 February 1859 Marian wrote to Sara Hennell, 'Our house is very comfortable...a tall cake, with a low garnish of holly and laurel.' She and Lewes were to live in Holly Lodge from 11 February 1859 until 24 September 1860.

What the Leweses did not foresee was that their denials would give Liggins a run. In their new home at Holly Lodge, South Fields, Wandsworth, where they had moved in February 1859, they heard from Sara Hennell that Mr Liggins, directly questioned, had declared that he had received no profit from *Adam Bede* but gave it all freely to Blackwood; and that a deputation of Dissenting parsons who had gone to Attleborough to ask Liggins to write for the *Eclectic* had found him, poor and servantless, washing his 'slop‑basin' (?slop‑pail) at the pump. Soon money was being collected to recompense Liggins for Blackwood's supposed shabbiness. Charles Newdegate, when he had met Blackwood the year before on Epsom Downs on Derby Day, had been certain that the author of *Scenes* was 'Liggers', and now, in April 1859, a Lincolnshire clergyman, Mr Henry Anders of Kirkby, wrote to *The Times* to confirm Liggins's authorship. Lewes, in the person of

'George Eliot', wrote a denial, but the story persisted and was accepted even by people as sensible as Mrs Gaskell. She, at least, wrote a handsome letter of apology to Marian when she learnt the truth, characteristically adding, 'I should not be quite true in my ending if I did not say before I concluded that I wish you *were* Mrs Lewes. However, that can't be helped, as far as I can see, and one must not judge others.' Only the gradual disclosure of George Eliot's true identity finally extinguished Liggins. He died in 1872 in the 'College' of *Amos Barton*, the workhouse of Chilvers Coton.

Before the provinces were convinced of George Eliot's identity, London had become reasonably sure, and with that assurance had come some of the unpleasantness the Leweses had feared, such as Hepworth Dixon's savage gossip paragraph in the *Athenaeum* in July 1859. The author of *Adam Bede*, he wrote, was obviously 'a clever woman with an observant eye and unschooled moral nature . . . a rather strong-minded lady, blessed with abundance of showy sentiment and a profusion of pious words, but kept for sale rather than for use. Vanish Eliot, Nicholas [a voucher for Liggins], Liggins, – enter, (let us say, at a guess,) Miss Biggins!'

The College for the Poor at Chilvers Coton was built in 1800 by French prisoners of war at the expense of Sir Roger Newdigate. 'Amos Barton has made his way through the sleet as far as the College, has thrown off his hat, cape, and boa, and is reading, in the dreary stone-floored dining-room, a portion of the morning service to the inmates seated on the benches before him.'

When identity could no longer be concealed, the Leweses had to make the best of a bad job, and this could not expediently be done by pleading the cruel social pressures Marian had been under. Indeed, it seemed best to deny that concealment had been attempted 'because there was any *fear* of the effect of the author's name. You may tell it openly to all', Lewes wrote to Barbara Bodichon, '. . . that the object of anonymity was to get the book judged on its own merits, and not prejudged as the work of a woman . . . they can't now unsay their admiration. . . .'

But they could. Readers felt they had been deceived, and what disturbed many people more than the author's immorality was her morality. What they had supposed, in a moralistic writer, to be a conventional Christian ethic must, in the translator of Strauss and Feuerbach, be nothing of the kind, and Crabbe Robinson, then eighty-four years old, spoke for many when he said that this, coupled with the author's sexual relationship, 'destroys all comfort-able notions of right and wrong, true and false'. Typical of the new assessments then felt necessary was that of an anonymous writer in a Methodist journal, the *London Quarterly*, some two years after the publication of *Adam Bede*. He con-demned the book as immoral, as 'a minute unhealthy analysis of feelings and impulses, to which the action of the will is made subordinate'.

All such detractions Lewes strove desperately to keep from Marian. From the earliest communications with Blackwood, Lewes had warned him never to write George Eliot an unsympathetic or overly critical word. 'Entre nous let me hint that unless you have any *serious* objection to make to Eliot's stories, *don't* make any. He is so easily discouraged, so diffident of himself –.' The 'entre nous' warning was constantly and widely repeated. Thus, to end the letter quoted above to Barbara Bodichon, the only friend who guessed at *Adam Bede*'s authorship with sufficient assurance to send congratulations, Lewes wrote, 'P.P.S. *Entre nous*. Please don't write or tell Marian anything *unpleasant* that you hear unless it is important for her to hear it. She is so very sensitive, and has such a tendency to dwell on and believe in unpleasant ideas that I always keep them from her.' He established the habit of coming down to breakfast before Marian and censoring her post, and any reviews less than effusive he tried to conceal – but somehow she always managed to see them and be distressed by them. He would beg Blackwood to send praise, which was 'like a *dram*' to her, as she herself recognized. 'I perceive that I have not the characteristics of the "popular author"', she wrote to Blackwood, 'and yet I am much in need of the warmly expressed sympathy which only popularity can win.'

Of all the pothers over *Adam Bede*, none, perhaps, caused Marian more distress than the local identifications inevitably made as soon as her authorship was known. Isaac had been heard to say early on that 'no one but his Sister could write the book' and that 'there were things in it about his father that she must have written'. Adam Bede was universally recognized as a portrait of Robert Evans, who was still remembered in Ellastone as one who, though 'rather lifted up and peppery-like', would push a younger workman aside and take his place in heaving a weight of timber, saying, 'Let it alone, lad! Thee'st got too much gristle i' they bones yet', who had learnt his letters from

To my dear husband, George Henry Lewes.
I give this MS. of a work which would never have been written but for the happiness which his love has conferred on my life.

Marian Lewes
March 23. 1859

The first volume was written at Richmond, the second at Munich & Dresden, the third at Richmond again. The work was begun on the 22d October 1857, & finished on the 16th November 1859. A large portion of it was written twice, though often scarcely at all altered in the copying; but other parts only once, & among these the description of Dinah & a good deal of her sermon, the love-scene between her & Seth, "Hetty's World", most of the scene in the Two Bedchambers, the talk between Arthur & Adam, various parts in the second volume which I can recall less easily, & in the third, Hetty's journeys, her confession, & the cottage scenes.

à propos of a particular case. The principle is this: never tell her anything that other people say about her books, for good or evil; unless of course it be to her something exceptionally gratifying & then something you know to please her apart from its being praise. She would like to know for instance when you or Mrs Bray sympathize with & like her books. But even this sh'd be conveyed only in a general intimation. You can tell me any details (& in a photism in all that concerns her), tho' I never look after what is said about myself favourable or unfavourable; but for her let her mind be as much as possible fixed on her art & not on the public.

I have not time [to] read over what is written but commend it to your interpretation. Ever yours
G. H. Lewes

a schoolmaster called, in life as in fiction, Bartle Massey; who had been the boyhood friend of the squire's son who had, the *Staffordshire Advertiser* revealed when listing real-life correspondences, got a local girl into trouble. Robert's brother Samuel was accepted as the original of Seth; and his wife Elizabeth, the former Methodist preacher who had prayed all night with the girl in the condemned cell, irrefutably as Dinah. Elizabeth Evans had died in 1849, her husband in the year of *Adam Bede*'s publication, and the memorial tablet to them set up in the Wesleyan Chapel in Wirksworth in 1873 unequivocally makes the identifications.

Again, as in *Scenes*, little trouble was taken in disguising many names: 'Oakbourne' is Ashbourne, 'Eagledale' is Dovedale, 'Norbourne' is Norbury, 'Rosseter' is Rocester.

Once initial correspondences were noted, others were eagerly sought, some plausible, some ridiculous. Though Robert Evans's father died at his son William's house in Ellastone in 1830 at the age of ninety, he has been widely named as the original of 'Thias Bede' – but it is tempting to substitute his eldest son George, who took to drink and died young. Francis Newdigate I has been cast for skinflint Squire Donnithorne, partly supported by the views

Each of Marian's manuscripts was bound for her by Blackwood and then presented with an inscription to her 'husband'; that of *Adam Bede* (*left*) is in red russia leather.

(*Right*) Letter to Sara Hennell from G. H. Lewes (12 September 1862), warning Sara never to tell Marian what people say about her books, unless it is 'something exceptionally gratifying'.

of an anonymous Nuneaton diarist who in 1835 rejoiced in his death as that of 'a despisable character – a bad unfeeling Landlord', but there does not appear to be any other evidence that fits Francis I to the skinflint Squire. The Donnithorne mansion may have been in part based on Wootton Hall; its sloping lawn is similar to the one described by Rousseau, and the Hermitage could conceivably have been his grotto; it is called 'an hermitage' in a contemporary letter. But near-by Ilam Hall could also provide a sloping lawn and a sequestered grotto (in which Congreve had written plays) and a large square central hall to the house; it had been rebuilt in 1834, and the younger William Evans, Marian's cousin, was the builder. There were cloisters at Croxden Abbey, only a few miles from Ellastone, and cloisters too at still nearer Calwich Abbey, where there had been an irascible squire and a disinherited heir. In *Adam Bede*, George Eliot had begun to meld her portraits of people and places with pictures made up of parts.

It would, of course, always have been impossible to deny that Elizabeth's night in Nottingham Jail had been an inspirational spark – between Marian and Lewes the book was known as 'My Aunt's Story' – but even more insulting than the suggestion that Mrs Poyser's racy talk was reproduced, not invented, Marian found the persistent accusation that Dinah's sermons had been taken from Elizabeth's and not made up by George Eliot. She came to be outraged by all suggestions that life had served as a model for *Adam Bede*. '*There is not a single portrait in Adam Bede* . . . Dinah and Seth are *not* my aunt and uncle. . . . The whole course of the story in Adam Bede – the descriptions of scenery or houses – the characters – the dialogue – *everything* is a combination from widely sundered elements of experience. . . . Treddleston is *not* Ellastone. Hayslope is, with a difference.' This letter, of 19 September 1859, was written to Charles Bray, who had been 'assisting' C. H. Bracebridge, the busybody of Florence Nightingale's Crimean journey, with researches into the originals of the book. The letter went on to deny knowledge of her aunt's having kept a journal – 'I don't believe she *could* write,' Marian told Blackwood – and of any knowledge of the Derbyshire/Staffordshire dialect except in so far as she might have heard it from her father and, on rare occasions, not 'so many times as I can count fingers', from his brothers.

In later years George Eliot was to be more frank, especially on the last point. In a letter to W. W. Skeat, published in the *English Dialect Society's Bibliographical List* of 1873, she states that 'the dialect in Adam B. . . . is modelled on the talk of North Staffordshire and the neighbouring part of Derbyshire'. She tended more and more to admit to intimate acquaintance with Ellastone, and once told Oscar Browning that the elder tree, described as growing over the carpenter's shop, was an early recollection, closely connected with the poetry of her life.

There was one disclosure of identity that Marian had looked forward to making, and this was to Sara Hennell and the Brays. Charles Bray had retired in 1856, when the ribbon trade was in the doldrums, and his consequently halved income of now only £400 a year had forced him to sell Rosehill to John Cash, who had married Mary Sibree. In 1857, the Brays moved to Ivy Cottage, next door to Rosehill, where Sara had been living with her mother

The memorial tablet to Mrs Samuel Evans (1776–1849) in the Ebenezer Wesleyan Chapel, Wirksworth.

Charles Bray (1811–84). 'You are the dearest, oldest, stupidest, tiresomest, delightfullest, and never-to-be-forgotten-est of friends to me – and I am ever Your affectionate Marian.' (*Letters*, 17 January 1853.)

CRYSTAL PALACE.

Thursday, May 21, 1863

PROGRAMME.

One o'clock.

ORCHESTRAL BAND OF THE COMPANY,

IN THE CONCERT ROOM.

1. MARCH, "Schiller" .... *Gross.*
2. OVERTURE, "Il Flauto Magico" ...... *Mozart.*
3. WALTZ, "Straussfedern" .... *Fahrbach.*
4. ARIA, "Stradella" .... *Flotow.*
5. SELECTION, "Il Trovatore" .... *Verdi.*
6. POLKA, "Impromptu" .... *Schulhoff.*
7. OVERTURE, "Euryanthe" .... *Weber.*

A. MANNS, CONDUCTOR.

[*Turn over.*

Programme for a concert at the Crystal Palace, which had been moved from Hyde Park to Sydenham in 1854; the sketches may be by Cara Bray or Sara Hennell.

since 1851. In 1859 Charles Bray built a small house, Charleston Villa, at Lawrie Park, Sydenham, where they were henceforth to live for part of each year to enjoy the concerts at the near-by Crystal Palace, hoping, though too often failing, to let the house for the rest of the time. When, however, the Brays, with Sara, came to Sydenham in June 1859 for the Handel Festival, it was to lodgings, and they invited the Leweses to dinner there on 20 June after a performance of the *Messiah*, the first time Marian had met Cara and Sara since 1854. That evening Marian revealed her literary identity, to, it appeared, their total astonishment. What she had not known was that Sara too had had special hopes of this meeting, eagerly looking forward to discussing the manuscript of her own new book with Marian as in the old days. Sara dined next day at Holly Lodge with the Leweses, apparently leaving her manuscript with them, and two days later, when she came again with the Brays, the Leweses felt compelled to tell Sara that they thought poorly of the manuscript. She was 'in strong stericks' all the way back to Coventry, Bray wrote to Marian, and he intimated that in future to refrain from serious criticism would be kinder. 'I *don't believe she can do better* and if she likes to amuse herself and spend her money in publishing, she can afford it and she does no one any harm.' The same post brought Marian a pathetic letter from Sara herself, recognizing humbly and with resignation that equality of friendship was henceforward lost.

At Holly Lodge, Marian was apt to wear, as Blackwood noted, 'a vexed anxious look'. It is hard to see why the Leweses had moved to a house they did not care for in a more urban district, when town life pressed so hardly on Marian and gave her so little. 'The wide sky, the *not*-London, makes a new creature of me in half an hour. . . . I come back to London, and again the air is full of demons', she wrote typically to Barbara in 1863. A usual day at Wandsworth would be spent in working all morning, luncheon at half past one, a walk in the afternoon, dinner at half past six and then, if Lewes was home, in reading aloud or with music, ever-increasingly a refreshment and a necessity to them both. But Marian spent many evenings alone while Lewes dined out, for she was not socially accepted.

One invitation Marian received on her own behalf was from Charles Edward Mudie, the owner of Mudie's Select Library. Despite his earlier incredulity that *Adam Bede* should have sprung from 'a polluted source', he sent Mr and Mrs Lewes a card to the reception he gave on 17 December 1860, for the move from his Bloomsbury premises to the Great Hall in New Oxford Street. Only Lewes accepted, though few people had a greater right to be there than George Eliot. For her novel-writing fell in the 'three-decker' period, when nearly all novels were first issued in three volumes at a retail price of 31s 6d. Almost all this first edition was sold to circulating libraries, and supremely to Mudie's; and it was through the libraries that almost all middle-class readers obtained the new novels. If they bought novels, it was a year or so after first publication, when cheap editions at about 12s and later at lower and lower prices were issued. In a letter of 1872, Lewes instances to Blackwood as typical, rich Mrs John Cash who, failing to obtain the newly issued numbers of *Middlemarch* from the library, saw no recourse but to borrow them from the Brays.

So, partly from choice, largely from necessity, Marian lived a withdrawn life. She found one friend in Wandsworth, Maria Congreve, daughter of the Coventry surgeon, Mr Bury, who had attended Robert Evans in his last illness. Maria had remembered Marian from Foleshill, and, outraged by the convention which let society accept Lewes while rejecting Marian, decided to call. A lasting friendship ensued, and Maria wrote to Marian that she had often thought that if Marian had remained in Coventry, she, Maria, would have gone to her with all her troubles as to no one else. Women were often to feel this about Marian throughout her life and after it, and 'I feel I could have told her all my troubles' is still to be heard from those who offer George Eliot the woman veneration as to a dead saint.

The party held in December 1860 to celebrate the opening of Mudie's Great Hall in New Oxford Street, London.

But on the Positivist philosophy of August Comte, the prime passion of Maria's husband Richard, there was disagreement. From about 1840 Positivism had been a general interest in the group to which the Leweses belonged. Comte's basic proposition, that not only knowledge but also moral values must be based on the methods and discoveries of the physical sciences, was one that must appeal to them. Spencer was interested, and so was J. S. Mill and, through him, Lewes, who at one time was an avowed Comtist, and played a part in making Comte's doctrines known in England. Many people hoped that Positivism might be the needed replacement for Christianity, but its eventual 'Religion of Humanity', which has been described as 'Catholicism without Christianity', was such as the Leweses could not accept. Many efforts were made, not least by Congreve, to enlist George Eliot in the cause, and her only good poem, 'O may I join the choir invisible' of 1867, was often spoken of as a Positivist hymn. But 'I cannot submit my intellect or my soul to the guidance of Comte', she was to say, and, as Haight remarks, her annual subscription to the Comte Fund of £5 'scarcely qualifies George Eliot as a pillar of Positivism'. The name she accepted and believed – mistakenly – she had invented for her own position was *meliorism*, the belief, as O.E.D. puts it, 'which affirms that the world may be made better by rightly-directed human effort'.

The Leweses loathed having people to stay, and deliberately kept an uncomfortable spare room. Only Barbara was generally welcome, Sara usually put off with an excuse. They were, however, happy to board the Congreves' dog Rough while the Congreves were abroad, and Marian, writing about him to Blackwood, confided that what she really wanted was a

The Pugs' Tea-Party, given at
Baginton on 30 May 1850 by Mrs
William Davenport Bromley's Smut
and Julia.

pug. Pugs were then enormously fashionable (had Fanny Houghton, before
the rupture, told Marian about the pugs' tea-party given at Baginton in 1850
by Mrs Davenport Bromley?). They were correspondingly hard to come by,
but Blackwood enlisted a cousin with sporting connections who jumped into
a hansom and eventually procured a pug from the cellar of a pugilistic East
End pub. He cost thirty guineas, 'but "Adam Bede" flourishes, so I grins
and bears it', said Blackwood. Pug was 'transcendent in ugliness. . . . Stupid
as a beauty; but very gentle, and affectionate', said Lewes, who even took him
to see Agnes. He was adored by Marian, but lost to the disconsolate family by
June 1861, presumably stolen, the then usual fate of superior London dogs.
He was succeeded by Ben, a bull terrier (*fl.* 1864–*c.* 1868), and Ben by Dash,
a dark brown spaniel who arrived in January 1872 and in February was lost.

At first, however, it did not look as if Pug would be such a good invest-
ment as Blackwood had hoped. In October 1859 he had sent Marian not
only the final payment of £400 on *Adam Bede*, but promise of an extra £800
in view of the book's success. Marian's acknowledgment, in a few cool lines,
gave Blackwood 'a fit of disgust'. His Edinburgh manager, George Simpson,

G. H. Lewes with Pug, 1859. 'Pug grows fatter and more fascinating every day,' Lewes wrote to his sons on 10 November, 'but his intellect does not develope [*sic*]. He is decidedly no genius.'

'Mr Blackwood sent me...a china *pug* as a memorial of my flesh and blood Pug, lost about a year ago', Marian wrote in her Journal on 1 January 1862. This second Pug's survival was revealed only in 1972 when Mrs Ouvry, Charles Lewes's youngest daughter, gave it to G. S. Haight, who generously suggested it should make its first public appearance here.

suspected what had happened: 'G.E. has sold herself to the highest bidder. I said very early that he was an avaricious soul.'

Marian was clearly planning her new novel as early as January 1859, when her Journal indicates she was looking in the *Annual Register* for cases of inundation. The germ of the new book's ending may have derived from family accounts of the flooding of the Dove at Ellastone. According to William Pitt's *General View of the Agriculture of the County of Stafford* of 1808, this river 'sometimes rises so high in twelve hours as to carry off sheep and cattle. A sudden rain is sufficient to inundate huge breadths of land near this river: as the declivity or fall is great, the swell of water is sudden.' But Marian would not have wished to base a new book on this district so soon after *Adam Bede*.

With a break to write a sadly poor supernatural story, 'The Lifted Veil', which made use of the old synagogue at Prague, Marian worked at the new novel through the move to Holly Lodge, and through an unsuccessful holiday in North Wales, marred by the crowds of summer tourists. On the way back they stopped at Lichfield to see Chrissey's daughters, Emily and

71

Katie, who were at school there. Chrissey had resumed touch with Marian on 24 February 1859. On 15 March she had died of consumption, and few of her nine children lived their normal span or enjoyed good health during their lives. Of the two little girls, Emily, whose pencilled note told Marian of Chrissey's death, had been deaf since childhood, and Katie was to die the next year. There is a letter of Marian's of 1860 to Miss Eborall, who ran the school, enclosing a cheque for clothes bought, at her request, for Emily, who remained a protégée. She stayed with the Leweses during the Christmas holidays of 1860.

From Lichfield the Leweses went to Weymouth, examining the rivers there and at Dorchester to see if they might meet the current fictional needs. These rivers did not, and it was not until September, in Lincolnshire, that they found that the Trent could provide the Floss, and Gainsborough, St Ogg's.

Blackwood had been kept in touch with the progress of this as yet untitled novel ('Sister Maggie'? The House of Tulliver'? 'The Tulliver Family'?) and had naturally supposed it to be his. The Leweses were not so sure. They wanted more money and Lewes, so Blackwood believed, discreetly let it be known that George Eliot was in the market. Smith, Elder, the London publishers, nibbled, and so did Samuel Lucas, editor of *Once a Week*, and so did Charles Dickens, who had dined at Holly Lodge in November and wanted George Eliot for *All the Year Round*. Blackwood maintained, with justification, that his offer of £3,000 for four years' copyright was fair. In the end the Leweses could not better it and were obliged to retreat to the affronted Blackwood, who was won over, not for the last time, by Marian herself. 'She is a fine character – all my former good opinion of her is restored. I am sure I cannot be mistaken both in her language and the expression of her face.' But Simpson's comment was 'I fear L. is not highminded.'

It was in 1859, before the new novel was finished, that Marian Lewes became a mother. When Lewes had eloped to Germany with her in 1854, his own sons Charles, Thornie and Bertie were aged twelve, ten, and eight, and the two eldest were at a school in Bayswater. In 1856 Lewes took them, and in 1857 Bertie too, to a school near Berne recommended by Sara Hennell, the Hofwyl School run on Pestalozzian principles. Henceforward, whenever the Leweses were in the neighbourhood, George Lewes would go to see them, but they had not yet met Marian and remained a part of Agnes's family. Now they were to belong to George and Marian. We do not know if this was settled at the time of the initial separation or, as Halcott Glover's fiction presents it, suddenly imposed on Agnes, but in July 1859 Lewes went to see the boys and 'I unburthened myself about Agnes to them. They were less distressed than I had anticipated and were delighted to hear about Marian.' The next summer, on the way back from Italy, both Leweses called at the school and the boys met their new mother, henceforward to be Mutter, Mütterchen, the Little Mother, or Mater. (It is pleasant to think that George Eliot was called Mater three or four years before O.E.D. records this use of English matrons better entitled.) They brought Charles back to England with them, and at Holly Lodge he found his own 'Nursie', Mrs Bell, who had come from Campden Hill to look after Pug and stayed to cherish her boys. In August 1860,

The sons of George and Agnes Lewes: Charles Lee (1842–91), Thornton Arnott (1844–69) and Herbert Arthur (1846–75).

recommended by Anthony Trollope and coached by Lewes and Marian, Charles entered the Post Office by its new competitive examination. Thornie came home in September and was taken by Lewes to a family in Edinburgh to be coached for the East Indian service; this later giving rise to rumours that Marian had had a son by Chapman who had been brought up in Edinburgh. Bertie stayed at Hofwyl till 1863, then was trained in farming, first in Scotland, later in Warwickshire. From 1860, 'our three great boys' are as persistent in Marian's letters as 'my husband' had been.

The new novel's title had been settled by Blackwood. Marian was doubtful of it. First, the Mill wasn't strictly on the Floss but on a small tributary; and then 'the title is of rather laborious utterance', an odd objection, since its rhythm is that of so many best-sellers from *Wuthering Heights* to *Gone with the Wind*. But Marian's ear for verbal rhythm was never very sure, and in 1871 she was to disconcert Tennyson by asking if he found as useful as she did Professor Sylvester's 'laws for verse making' (*The Laws of Verse*, 1870, by the mathematician James Sylvester). 'I can't understand that,' said Tennyson.

The Mill on the Floss was published on 4 April 1860, when the Leweses were in Rome; they were to make a practice of being out of the country when Marian's books came out. Six thousand copies were sold in the first seven weeks, but the reviews were mixed, and there can be no doubt that knowledge of the author's identity affected some reviewers. If most readers were charmed by the country childhoods, and lovers of Mrs Poyser delighted by the aunts, some critics were now on the alert for immorality, and, in the relations between Maggie Tulliver and Stephen Guest, some of them found it. The anonymous critic of the *Saturday Review* observed that Stephen kissing Maggie's arm was not 'a theme that a female novelist can touch on without leaving a feeling of hesitation, if not repulsion, in the reader. . . . There are emotions over which we ought to throw a veil'; and Swinburne some years

73

A wide plain, where the broadening Floss hurries on between its green banks to the Northern Sea, & the loving tide, rushing to meet it checks its passage with an impetuous embrace. On this mighty tide the black ships — laden with the fresh-scented fir-planks, with rounded sacks of oil-bearing seed, or with the dark glitter of coal — are borne along to the town of St Ogg's, which shows its aged, fluted red roofs & the broad gables of its wharves between the green banks & the river-brink, tinging the water with a soft purple hue under the transient glance of the February sun. Far away on each hand stretch the rich pastures, & the patches of dark earth made ready for the seed of broad-leaved green crops, or touched already with the tint of the tender-bladed autumn-sown corn. There is a remnant still of the last year's golden clusters of bee-hive ricks rising at intervals beyond the hedge-rows; & everywhere the hedge-rows are studded with trees; the distant ships seem to be lifting their masts & stretching their red-brown sails close among the branches of the spreading ash. Just by the red...

'"It is coming, Maggie!" Tom said, in a deep hoarse voice, loosing the oars and clasping her. The next instant the boat was no longer seen upon the water.' (*The Mill on the Floss*, Bk. VII, Ch. v.)

(*Right*) The first page of the manuscript.

later wrote that no man could encounter Stephen Guest without 'a twitching in his fingers and a tingling in his toes' as he longed to horsewhip or kick 'the cur'. The realism of the attraction between Maggie and Stephen offended many critics who, as Marian despairingly wrote to Blackwood, could not accept the ethically imperfect as art.

'If the ethics of art do not admit the truthful presentation of a character . . . *then*, it seems to me, the ethics of art are too narrow, and must be widened.'

When the game of identifications was inevitably played, she made few denials. She was Maggie – or rather, the young Maggie was the young Mary Ann. Isaac was Tom. Chrissey was Lucy. The Dobson sisters were the Pearson aunts, right down to Aunt Glegg's 'fuzzy front'. The garden, the pond, the Red Deeps, are all from memories of childhood at Griff. But the part played by memory was becoming less. Mr and Mrs Tulliver are not Mr

74

and Mrs Evans, and though identifications have been suggested for Philip Wakem (notably D'Albert, who was 'not more than 4 feet high with a deformed spine . . . but . . . a finely formed head') and for Stephen Guest, there are no longer the certainties that snapped characters in *Scenes* with real-life counterparts.

There is a reference to 'the Italian story you have in view' in a letter from Blackwood to Marian of June 1858. After this we hear no more of an Italian story until the summer visit to Italy in 1860, when at Florence it suddenly occurred to Lewes, as he wrote in his Journal, that the life and times of Savonarola 'afford fine material for an historical romance. Polly at once caught at the idea with enthusiasm.' But the season was still not ripe, for domestic duties were pressing. Charles's daily journeys to work from Wandsworth were long and tiring, and though Marian had taken trouble to prepare a pleasant room for him – presumably the once-uncomfortable spare room – Holly Lodge had no space for three sons. There could be no question of moving to the longed-for country now, unless Charles was to go into lodgings, and this was unthinkable. The affection that quickly developed between him and Marian was deep and lasting. Unable to find a satisfactory house to buy or rent, they stored their furniture and took for the time being furnished houses, first at 10 Harewood Square in September 1860, then moved just before Christmas to 16 Blandford Square which they had taken on a three-year lease. At the end of that time, they hoped, the boys would be settled, and the parents could live where they pleased.

Though Marian was now famous she was still socially unaccepted, and it was mostly men without their wives who called at Blandford Square. The Leweses were always 'at home' on Saturday evenings, and often the evenings were musical. Marian played the piano, Charles the violin, and friends contributed other strings. Herbert Spencer and Anthony Trollope were regular visitors, and one day Arthur Helps, since 1860 Clerk to the Privy Council, was able to tell Marian how much the Queen admired her books, and especially *The Mill on the Floss*. Marian found this 'extremely agreeable'; she had no doubt forgotten that when she had seen the Queen at the opera in 1852 she had found her 'deplorable . . . so utterly mean in contour and expression'. (Jane Austen had as readily forgotten her earlier contempt for the Prince Regent when he honoured her by accepting the dedication to *Emma*.) As George Lewes commented to his boys on another occasion, 'Dear mother! she thinks the admiration of royalty so much more complimentary than the admiration of other mortals.'

A chalk drawing was made of Marian at this time by Samuel Laurence, once an inhabitant of the Bayswater Philanstery. But the Leweses did not like the result, though its 'pensive sad look' seemed to Blackwood, who eventually bought it, exactly that of Marian when he had first met her. Poor Marian never did like any representations of herself. She begged the Brays not to display the photograph they had, and thereafter always denied that any photographs existed. A few had in fact been taken, notably by Mayall of Regent Street in 1858, and the Leweses had several copies but not for display. In 1867 she was denying that any portraits existed except the Laurence and a

'I have rather a horror of photography. Mayall took one a couple of years ago, and we have several copies of it on paper, but it is not thoroughly satisfactory.' (G.E. to Blackwood, 23 June 1860.) 'I have *no* photograph of myself, having always avoided having one taken.' (G.E. to Harriet Beecher Stowe, 24 June 1872.) Bessie Belloc declared that this photograph by Mayall of 1858 gave 'the only real indication left to us of the true shape of the head and of George Eliot's smile and general bearing'.

(*Right*) The portrait by Frederic Burton of 1865, which hung over the mantel in Lewes's study at the Priory.

crayon drawing by Frederic Burton of 1864–65; and this to Cara who had herself drawn Marian in the 1840s and must surely have seen the portrait by D'Albert. When people met Marian they were usually soon enraptured by her beautiful low voice and her expressive blue-grey eyes, but there is no denying that the plain girl had become an ugly woman. 'One rarely sees a plainer woman', said Charles Eliot Norton, with whom there was clearly lack of rapport; 'dull complexion, dull eye, heavy features.' Henry James found her 'magnificently ugly – deliciously hideous' but in this ugliness there was a charm that ravished – 'Behold me literally in love with this great horse-faced blue-stocking.' Equine comparisons were often made, their apotheosis that of the humorist 'Timothy Shy' in the 1940s – 'an elderly Jewish cab-horse with ringlets'. But John Morley told Elizabeth Haldane that with dignity and a sad expression, George Eliot looked 'bishop-like'.

'I am engaged now in writing a story, the idea of which...has thrust itself between me and the other book I was meditating. It is "Silas Marner, the Weaver of Raveloe".' (G.E.'s Journal, 28 November 1860.) The first page of the manuscript.

The new book born in Florence was delayed not only by domestic duties but also by other writing. In the summer of 1860 Marian had written a short story, called first 'Mr David Faux, Confectioner', then 'The Idiot Brother', and finally, when published in the *Cornhill* in 1864, 'Brother Jacob'. Blackwood, with a sternness unusual in his dealings with this sensitive author, advised her in 1866 to omit this and 'The Lifted Veil' from the recognized series of her works – 'They are both as clever as can be, but there is a painful want of light about them.' Both were, none the less, sold to America and to Tauchnitz, and they were included in the 1879 Cabinet Edition of George Eliot's Works. Then suddenly, it seemed, a compulsive idea thrust itself forward, an idea based, Marian said, on a glimpse she had once had of an itinerant weaver with his bag on his back. This was *Silas Marner*, finished in March 1861, published on 2 April in a one-volume edition at 12*s*. The only presentation copy sent was to George Lewes's mother, Mrs Willim, who had accepted Marian after the move to Blandford Square as '*your amiable Wife*'.

Almost all the reviewers were delighted – and relieved. George Eliot had retreated from the questionable indelicacies of *The Mill* to a novel that the *Saturday Review* typically considered 'as good as *Adam Bede*, except that it is shorter'. The 'scene at the Rainbow' in Chapter VI displaced Mrs Poyser

as the prototype of all that faithful novel-readers most admired in George Eliot's work, though for a few hostile critics this scene could stand for the 'realism' of bucolic coarseness they deplored in an art form whose duty was, they felt, to portray the ideal. *Silas Marner* is the only one of George Eliot's English-set novels in which real-life resemblances have not been traced. Mathilde Blind, who wrote a good life of George Eliot in 1883, pointed out that *Silas Marner* markedly resembles *Jermola the Potter* by the popular Polish novelist J. I. Kraszewski, and Anne Fremantle says the two stories are 'identical'.

This is going rather far, but certainly there are resemblances more striking than Marian could have derived from any brief and casual account of the Polish novel's plot. But though this was published in 1857, it was not translated into any language Marian knew until after *Silas Marner* appeared. If it could be shown that she knew William Ralston Shedden-Ralston by this date, a reasonable guess would be that she had been told the story in the needed detail by him. Later a frequent visitor to the Leweses, Ralston worked at the British Museum, specializing in Slavonic studies and translations, and became well known as a public story-teller. His first recorded appearance with the Leweses is in May 1867, when his call at their home is noted as if he was already an habitué.

'A Scene from Silas Marner', exhibited in 1872 at the gallery of the Society of French Artists by Ford Madox Brown's son Oliver, a brilliantly promising painter and novelist, who died in 1874 aged nineteen. The scene is that of the close of Chapter XII.

79

'Enter Mutter (with her nose running and her feet well muffled). She imagines herself kissing her dearest Grub.... Pater has been pretty well until to-day, but now he has a bad sore throat.' Thus Marian to Charles Lewes on 5 May 1861, just after arrival in Florence. But their ills were only the 'Florentine grippe' and on 17 May she could tell Charles that 'Pater and I have had great satisfaction in finding our impressions of admiration more than renewed in returning to Florence'.

Before the book came out, the Leweses went abroad. This time they departed from their confirmed frugal habits and made their journey to Florence, via the Corniche road, in comfort and even luxury. Usually their travel arrangements, for two such fragile people, were deplorable. They never took the precaution of writing ahead for rooms, and the day, or often, night of arrival was apt to be spent in tramping around, searching for rooms until they fell, exhausted, into usually unsatisfactory beds, and next day had to start tramping and searching again.

But this time all was delight, and the *en-route* letters to Charles from Pater and Mater are full of joy. 'The most delightful (and the most expensive) journey we have ever had', they told Blackwood. Florence, however, was mostly hard work, with research in the Magliabecchian Library and excursions under the guidance of Thomas Adolphus Trollope, Anthony's brother, who unfortunately returned to Florence just as the Leweses were about to leave; and they gladly stayed on to take advantage of his profound knowledge of the city and neighbourhood.

But somehow the new book did not go. The title had been decided on: *Romola*, after a hill near Florence. But once the Leweses got home, Marian drowned herself ever deeper in research and found herself less and less able to 'see' her characters living, as previously she had always been able to do. 'Mind your care is to discountenance the idea of a Romance being the product of an Encyclopaedia', Lewes wrote worriedly to Blackwood, and a typical letter of Marian's to Tom Trollope shows what he meant:

Concerning *netto de specchio*, I have found a passage in Varchi which decides the point. . . . Concerning the Bardi, my authority for making them originally *popolani* is G. Villani. He says, c. xxix, *'e gia cominciavano . . . (etc.)* And c. lxxxi, *e questo furano le principale case . . . (etc.)* Concerning the phrase[s] *in piazza*, and *in mercato*, my choice of them was partly founded on the colloquial usage as represented by Sacchetti. . . .

And so on and so forth. With headaches and prostrations disabling beyond even Marian's habitual ills, she struggled on through the spring on 1862, and on 9 June could at last write in her Diary, 'Put the last stroke to *Romola*. *Ebenezer!*' In May, Blackwood had received a brief letter from her, telling him that she had had from elsewhere an offer for her novel 'handsomer than almost any terms ever offered to a writer of Fiction', and that, after various objections had been removed, she had accepted it.

'Elsewhere' was George Smith of Smith, Elder, who had been after George Eliot for some time. He wooed both Leweses with, it can fairly be said, cunning. First, a series of Lewes's natural-history pieces from the *Cornhill* were to be published in book form. Next, Lewes was offered the editorship of the magazine after Thackeray's resignation; he accepted, instead, the post of chief literary adviser at £600 a year. With these, the offer for *Romola*: £10,000 for the entire copyright – 'the most magnificent offer ever yet made for a novel', Lewes wrote in his Journal – with initial serial publication in the *Cornhill*, and illustrations by Frederic Leighton. ('Lewes is clever. Both were extremely polite to me; her I shall like much', Leighton wrote to his father after the first meeting.)

Blackwood, who had been to George Eliot a publisher such as writers dream of, behaved with great dignity. He allowed himself one sharp remark to the defecting author. 'I'm fully satisfied that it must have been a very sharp pang to you,' he said when she excused herself to him, and then, not wishing 'in her peculiar circumstances to hit her', he shook hands and came away. To his London manager, Joseph Langford, Blackwood wrote that, though the business stuck in his throat, he was sure she had acted against her own inclination, but that 'the voracity of Lewes' would have been hard to meet, so 'Let them go.' It cannot but have been gratifying to learn later what a poor bargain Smith had made. Whatever pressurizing part Lewes had played, Marian at least did not put money first. 'It is better for me not to be rich', she had written in her Journal on 23 January 1862, the day that Smith had asked if she was open to 'a magnificent offer', and she had insisted on accepting only £7,000 rather than extend the book to make the sixteen instalments he wanted; and when *Romola* failed of financial success, Marian gave her story 'Brother Jacob' to the *Cornhill* as a present, although Smith had offered to pay her 250 guineas for it.

Serial publication of *Romola* began in July 1862, and some friends, notably Anthony Trollope, Arthur Helps and Robert Browning, made some amiable comments; Lewes 'lost' a letter from Sara Hennell quoting adverse opinions. There were a few notices at the time, though most reviewers waited for the book publication on 6 July 1863, a month before the last instalment of the serialization. The general and enduring opinion was voiced by the

The Visible Madonna: Frederic Leighton's illustration to the chapter so called in *Romola* (Bk. III, Ch. xliv), beside Barbara Bodichon's satirical impression of herself with children.

Saturday Review: 'No reader of *Romola* will lay it down without admiration, and few with regret.' Oscar Browning stands almost alone in maintaining that this is George Eliot's greatest work. The *Westminster Review*, certainly, agreed, but may be considered a special case. What did impress almost all the reviewers was the book's deep moral tone. From its publication began a growing tendency to look on George Eliot as a great ethical teacher; and some people pointed out the physical likeness between George Eliot and Savonarola. No domestic portraits were claimed this time. It was Marian who revealed that Romola was based on Barbara Bodichon – 'noble-looking Barbara', as she had described her soon after they first met.

'Killed Tito in great excitement! – Went to see the Priory, North Bank', Marian wrote in her Diary on 16 May 1863. The new home was, after all, to be in London. North Bank ran beside the Regent's Park Canal between

Park Road and Grove End Road, St John's Wood, its site now covered by an electricity power-station. No. 21, the Priory, was a small square two-storey building with high brick walls surrounding a garden full of rose-bushes. The Leweses paid £2,000 for a forty-nine-year lease.

'Mr Owen Jones has undertaken the ornamentation of our drawing room and will prescribe all about chairs, etc. I think, after all, I like a clean kitchen better than any other room', Marian wrote to Sara. Neither she nor Mr Jones concerned themselves with the spare room which was, Cara was warned in 1867, uncomfortable; and a couple of years later Barbara was told that the bed was no softer or broader, though there was now a new carpet and a new piece of matting for the bath. The bed, apparently one discarded by Charles, was offered to Sara in 1869, but for only one night, 'for to have a visitor staying with us would be a perturbation of our lives which . . . we cannot endure.'

'We are really going to buy the Priory after all:–[Cara] would think it very pretty if she saw it now with the roses blooming about it.' (G.E. to Sara Hennell, 11 July 1863.)

The drawing-room of the Priory, hung with Leighton's drawings.

(*Right*) Titian's *The Tribute Money*, which Marian first saw in Dresden in 1858; she is said to have had the appearance of this Christ in mind as that of Daniel Deronda, whose face, as she described it in Ch. XL, was 'not more distinctively oriental than many a type seen among what we call the Latin races: rich in youthful health, and with a forcible masculine gravity in its repose'.

Owen Jones, the architect and designer and a friend of the Leweses, was then perhaps best known for his Alhambraesque features in the new Kensington Palace Gardens. George and Marian thought he had made 'a very exquisite thing' of the Priory, but visitors were not so sure. The rooms were cheerful, said Norton, and lined with well-filled bookcases, save over the study fireplace, 'where hung a staring likeness and odious, vulgarizing portrait of Mrs Lewes [that by Burton]. Indeed all the works of art in the house bore witness to the want of delicate artistic feeling, or good culture on the part of the occupants, with the single exception, so far as I observed, of the common lithograph of Titian's "Christ of the Tribute Money".' Admittedly, Norton was not sympathetic to the Leweses. Like many others, he found Marian's manner 'too intense, she leans over to you till her face is close to yours, and speaks in very low and eager tones . . . her manner . . . suggests that, of a woman who feels herself to be of mark and is accustomed, as she is, to the adoring flattery of a coterie of not undistinguished admirers.'

Many visitors to the Priory brought away similar impressions of Marian's public manner which henceforward grew upon her. The Leweses had moved on 1 November 1863, and on the 24th they combined a housewarming with a twenty-first birthday-party for Charles. Owen Jones had bent his talents to the hostess's appearance, and she was, as she wrote to Maria Congreve, 'splendid in a grey moire antique'. Among the guests were Herbert Spencer, E. S. Dallas of *The Times*, Robert Noel, the brother of Cara's friend Edward, with his wife, and Mrs Peter Taylor, she and her husband both liberal-minded reformers whom Marian had first met at 142 Strand. So ladies were not lacking, and neither was music, for Leopold Jansa, who was to give Marian lessons in accompaniment, played the violin. Charles brought Henry Buxton Forman, a colleague at the Post Office; of the forged 'private editions' of George Eliot's poems, 'Brother and Sister' and 'Agatha', purportedly of 1868 and 1869, Buxton Forman is now thought by both Haight and John Carter to have been the likely instigator of the latter.

Charles was settled and doing well. The other boys were more difficult. Thornton had failed his final examination for the Indian Service, and had no wish to try again. He wanted to go and fight with the Polish guerrillas against the Russians, and it was Barbara Bodichon who persuaded him there might be greater delights in shooting big game in Natal. So Thornton sailed for Durban, just before the Leweses moved into the Priory. In 1866, he obtained a grant of some 3,000 acres of land on the Orange River, and wrote home to urge that Bertie should come out and join him. Bertie was delighted at the prospect of putting his education in farming to practical use, and, armed by the Leweses with funds for the purchase of farm stock, he sailed in September 1866. By this time Charles, too, had left home. In 1865, he married Gertrude Hill, sister of Octavia Hill, and granddaughter and adopted daughter of Dr Southwood Smith, the well-known Unitarian minister.

The Annunciation, attributed to Titian, in the Scuola di San Rocco at Venice, which suggested the subject of *The Spanish Gypsy* – 'a great dramatic motive of the same class as those used by the Greek dramatists.' (*Notes on 'The Spanish Gypsy'.*)

Early in 1864 Marian had been rather whiling away the time than usefully working with a notion of an historical play set in Italy for Helen Faucit, an actress friend. The idea was Lewes's, the title of the play *Savello*, the attempt to write it unsuccessful. Another seemingly more promising idea presented itself in May 1864, when the Leweses were in Venice with Frederic Burton. In her Notes on *The Spanish Gypsy*, which is what the putative play became, Marian traced its origin to a Titian *Annunciation* seen in Venice: '"Behold the handmaid of the Lord." Here, I thought, is a subject grander than that of Iphigenia.' Having decided that no setting but Spain could suit the subject – perhaps the influence of Owen Jones? – Marian proceeded, with her usual thoroughness, to read up Spain. She worked hard through an autumn of ill-health for both, only slightly mitigated by cures at Harrogate and, for George, at Malvern. But the play would not go, and in February 1865 Marian wrote in her Journal, 'Ill and very miserable. George has taken my drama away from me.' In March she began *Felix Holt*.

This book took her fourteen months to write. A major difficulty was the extraordinarily complicated inheritance situation Marian needed, and for this she received constant help from her lawyer friend, the Positivist Frederic Harrison. He was untiring at devising the precise legal tangles required, his reward, he said, the knowledge that he had written at least one sentence that would endure in English literature. The first step in this inheritance tangle, the leaving of a substantial estate to A only for life, and then away from A's heirs to B and his heirs, is, incidentally, the situation created by Sir Roger Newdigate.

Lewes sent the manuscript to George Smith, asking £5,000 for the copyright. Smith declined it. The *Cornhill* had dropped circulation during *Romola*'s serialization, and Smith's huge payment for that copyright had not proved financially justified. There was nothing for it but to try Blackwood, which Lewes did, intimating that Blackwood was the first publisher he had

Among the objects in Coventry Public Library said to have belonged to George Eliot are this reading-lamp (*above*) and writing-case (*opposite*).

approached. Blackwood was happy to have his first-class passenger back, with a book he thought 'a perfect marvel', and for five years' copyright he readily gave £5,000. The old relationship was re-established, not to be broken again.

Lewes had given up his more or less nominal post on the *Cornhill* in October 1864, and had accepted the editorship, at £600 a year, of a new literary review, the *Fortnightly*, first issued in May 1865 and based on the *Revue des Deux Mondes*; it inaugurated a policy, new in English letters, of signed reviewing, and 'George Eliot' contributed two signed pieces to the first number. But George Smith then set on foot a project which excited Lewes more, and entailed less work, an important consideration in view of his increasingly poor health. This was the *Pall Mall Gazette*, an evening news-paper, and Lewes gave up the *Fortnightly* for advisory work on the *Gazette* at £300 a year.

Felix Holt, finished on 31 May 1866, was published on 15 June, the Leweses having, as usual, gone abroad just beforehand, this time to Holland, Belgium and Germany. Though the book did not sell as well as had been hoped, and Blackwood lost money on it, it was received by the critics with, on the whole, admiration and – after *Romola* – relief. But there were adverse criticisms of the novel's structure, and David Carroll in *George Eliot: The Critical Heritage* (1971), a collection of contemporary reviews, suggests that the critics at this point lacked criteria appropriate to the novels George Eliot was writing. The more intelligent of them, such as Dallas, had some apprecia-tion of the great subtlety with which the Jermyn-Transom relationship had been depicted, but could not help regretfully noting that 'There is no one personage in the book . . . so witty of speech as good old Mrs Poyser.'

Fanny Houghton's fears of further family representations were not, after all, realized; Nuneaton readers would, however, recognize the Reform Bill riots in their town, and Coventry readers in the Reverend Rufus Lyon the Reverend Francis Franklin, father of the Misses Franklin of Nantglyn School. 'The Book is marvellously clever: that you *must* confess', Fanny wrote to Isaac after she had read it – '*must* confess', despite Isaac's dislike of Radicals.

Marian had not started writing fiction until she was, in Edmund Gosse's words, 'a storm-tried matron of thirty-seven'. Now, ten years later, she was to give up fiction for three years while she devoted herself to verse. Her most constant inspiration was Wordsworth. He would, she believed, have liked *Silas Marner*, a work that would have been better suited, she felt, to 'metrical rather than to prose fiction'. This is a fearful thought, especially in view of the fact that in her metrical fiction, as Gosse wrote, 'occasionally she reproduces very closely the duller parts of *The Excursion*'. He suggests that she had come to realize that as a writer of imaginative prose her chief lack was that of poetic quality – 'It never sings.' It may well be that, after the failure of *Romola*, Marian believed this to be the case, and, if so, it could be a fatal lack in a writer whose avowed intention was ' – that of the *aesthetic*, not the doctrinal teacher – the raising of the nobler emotions, which make mankind desire the social right'.

However this may be, Marian gave herself to her verse, and it gripped her as forcefully as her prose fiction had done, a nice example of the insufficiently stressed truth that a creator's devotion to his inspiration is insufficient test of its worth. After some English and foreign holidays, and most notably a journey to Spain in early 1867, *The Spanish Gypsy* was finished in April 1868 and published in early June in an edition intended, as Simpson wrote to Blackwood, to be 'fit for a Drawing-Room Table'. Its theme, as foreshadowed in Venice in 1864, was that higher duty may deprive a woman of normal happiness, and its plot hinged, not for the first or last time in George Eliot's work, on mysterious parentage. The reviews were not fulsome; and this time we find Lewes showing Marian a thoroughly nasty one from the *Pall Mall Gazette*; that in the *Spectator*, which described *The Spanish Gypsy* as 'the greatest poem . . . which has ever proceeded from a woman', Marian found 'modest in tone'.

With, presumably, after its publication in 1870, the continued help of Professor Sylvester's *The Laws of Verse*, Marian plodded on with 'Agatha', 'How Lisa Loved the King', 'The Legend of Jubal', 'Armgart', and, with perpetual revision, at the autobiographical sonnet sequence, 'Brother and Sister'. When the manuscript of reprints and new poems reached Blackwood in 1874, he wrote to the author, 'They are truly good and have their meaning' ('Other readers', Haight comments, 'have been as hard pressed as Blackwood to find something to say about them'), and, 'If you have any lighter pieces written before the sense of what a great author should do for mankind came so strongly upon you, I should like much to look at them.'

Only one prose work was published in this period. 'The Address to Working Men, by Felix Holt', a suggestion of Blackwood's, was published in *Maga* of January 1868, its occasion the passing of the Second Reform Bill in 1867. Its view, that education rather than the vote was the remedy for working-class ills, was Marian's and Blackwood's; we do not hear of a working-class response. 'Young men . . . are the class I most care to please', Marian had written to Blackwood the year before, but it was soon to be undergraduates rather than working men whom she sought to influence.

Marian did not begin writing a new novel until August 1869, and the gap in her important working life provides the opportunity to catch up with her life in her circle.

With her family, Marian's contacts were almost non-existent. 'I cling strongly to kith and kin, even though they reject *me*', she wrote to Barbara in 1869 – but did she? Had the obsessive yearning towards Isaac really survived childhood, and would Marian really now have welcomed resumption of family relations? Young Robert Evans, who had written in 1864 to tell Marian of his father's death, wrote again in 1866 to invite her and Mr Lewes to visit him and his wife in Nottingham. Such a visit would undoubtedly have provided an opportunity to meet at least Fanny Houghton again; she was now widowed and living with Robert's mother. But Marian did not accept. In 1874 Isaac's elder daughter Edith called at the Priory with her husband, the Reverend William Griffiths of St Nicholas, Birmingham, and Marian no doubt heard such family news as that Isaac's eldest son Frederic had gone into

'This finest portrait of George Eliot,' writes G. S. Haight; 'The full, well-formed lips reveal the powerful sensual element noted by those who knew her intimately. Mathilde Blind said of it that it failed to convey either "the infinite depth of her observant eye" or "that cold, subtle, and unconscious cruelty of expression which might occasionally be detected".' Samuel Laurence painted the original in 1860, but the Leweses did not like it ('perhaps it was too revealing?' suggests Haight); it was given to Blackwood but has now been lost. The preliminary sketch, reproduced here, now hangs in Girton College; it is misdated 1857.

the Church, and that the second son Walter was following his father's and grandfather's profession in Newdigate employ. But though the Griffiths were kindly received, they were apparently not pressed to come again. Marian kept touch only with Chrissey's Emily, for whom she had assumed responsibility. Emily lived, unmarried, in Brighton, and not infrequently visited and was visited by the Leweses; she was to be one of the few legatees of Marian's will.

Barbara Bodichon and, to a lesser extent, Bessie Belloc remained friends throughout, though Bessie's daughter, Mrs Belloc Lowndes, was sometimes inclined to play this down. Although part of Barbara's time was spent in Algiers with her distinctly eccentric husband, she remained active and influential in women's movements. To her is owed in no small measure the founding of Girton College in 1869 and the passing of the Married Women's Property Acts, of which the first was in 1870; and she was enthusiastic for Women's Suffrage. Marian's sympathy with Barbara's causes was limited. Though she was one of the 24,000 signers of the petition for the Married Women's Property Bill of 1857, she did not join the Kensington Society

Barbara Bodichon, who, said her biographer, 'played L'Allegro to George Eliot's Il Penseroso'. Attacked by hemiplegia while sketching in Cornwall in 1878, Barbara bravely endured many years of disability and died at the generously hospitable house she had built, Scalands, in Sussex.

where Barbara discussed women's higher education and like issues with such women as Emily Davies, Sophia Jex-Blake, Elizabeth Garrett, Helen Taylor, and Miss Buss and Miss Beale. From the time Marian became known and successful, she and Lewes were preternaturally careful of her public reputation or, as we should say her image, and identification with unconventional causes such as Women's Suffrage – 'an extremely doubtful good' she wrote to Sara – was not for her. She was, however, sympathetic to women's education, believing that women should be 'educated equally with men, and secured . . . from suffering the exercise of unrighteous power.' At Barbara's request, Marian allowed Emily Davies to call on her in November 1867, for 'some conversation on the desirable project of founding a College for women', though afterwards she felt compelled to write to Miss Davies to apologize for having 'talked on serious subjects in a sadly flurried imperfect way'. Though Laurence's sketch for her portrait now hangs in Girton, she can be considered only a moderate benefactor of that college. She sent £50 'From the Author of *Romola*', but replied only cautiously to further requests for money.

Times became increasingly hard for the Brays. In July 1860 Marian had, probably providently, refused to invest money in a hopeful venture of Charles's. 'At present I have no money that I could invest', she wrote to him, though in November she was able to put £2,000 in East Indian stocks and expected shortly to put in £2,000 more. The next year the Brays had to leave Ivy Cottage for a still smaller house in Barr's Hill Terrace on the outskirts of Coventry, and Marian begged to be allowed to give personal help – she could easily spare £100, she said – but this was refused. Lewes was always impatient with 'that hotbed of priggishness', as Gosse saw the Brays, but his attitude did not make easier for Marian the always painful process of growing away from former friends. In 1860 Lewes wrote a gratuitously cruel letter to Sara, pulling her work to pieces by standards so exacting as to be irrelevant to her, and forgetting or ignoring Charles's plea, 'She cannot do better.' Sara was deeply pained by both the Leweses' comments on her book, and Marian begged, 'Do not write again upon opinions on large questions, dear Sara.' And in 1866, when Charles's book, *Force and its Mental and Moral Correlates*, came out, 'Mr G. H. Lewes, although hitherto well-disposed towards me, refused to notice [it], on the ground that I had used "Force" in a different sense to that which it had hitherto been used by men of science.' It was an especially bad time for the Brays in that their adopted daughter Nellie, who had always been difficult, had died the year before. But Lewes's refusal to notice the book was probably kinder than his review could truthfully have been.

From about 1863 Marian had had to become used to being recognized, accosted, furtively touched, asked for autographs whenever she appeared in public, which, consequently, she did as little as possible. Lewes's protection was unfailing. He dealt with her considerable fan mail – the schoolgirl who wanted critical comment on her school exercises, the lady who wanted to know what terms to ask of a publisher – and, when travelling, he would look through the Visitors' Lists at the resorts, to see if privacy was likely to be invaded, before deciding on a stay; though at Petersthal in July 1868, he could not resist revealing himself as *the* Mr Lewes 'to a very pretty, cultured and charming girl' whom he sat next to at dinner. He was now fairly *the* Mr Lewes without reference to George Eliot. In scientific circles his reputation was high as an able vigorous communicator, and his scientific interests, and the social life he had retained with his own circle of friends, not infrequently took him away from home, as did the various 'cures' he tried for his poor health. During his absences, Marian comported herself with the utmost caution. To Maria Congreve, who had invited her to a concert in 1867, when George was away, she explained that 'Mr Lewes objected, on grounds which I think just, to my going to any public manifestation without him, since [the reason for] his absence could not be divined by outsiders.'

People who met Lewes for the first time in the ambience of George Eliot did not, on the whole, take to him, and a fair summation of the general impression he made is Norton's:

He looks and moves like an old-fashioned French barber or dancing-master, very ugly, very vivacious, very entertaining. . . . His talk is much more French than English in its liveliness and in the grimace and gesture with which it is accompanied,

– all the action of his mind is rapid, and it is so full that it seems to be running over. 'Oh, if you like to hear stories', he said one day, 'I can tell you stories for twelve hours on end' – it is just the same if you like to hear science, or philosophy. His acquirements are very wide, wider, perhaps, than deep; but the men who know most on special subjects speak with respect of his attainments. I have heard both Darwin and Sir Charles Lyell speak very highly of the thoroughness of his knowledge in their departments. . . . But he is not a man who wins more than a moderate liking from you. He has the vanity of a Frenchman; his moral perceptions are not acute and he consequently often fails in social tact and taste. He has what it is hard to call a vulgar air, but at least there is something in his air which reminds you of vulgarity.

This was written after Norton's first visit to the Priory in 1869. After the move there in 1863, a new social policy was decided upon, and the famous Sunday afternoons inaugurated. Unwritten rules were strictly applied. Women would not be invited but could ask to come. Though no one spoke of Mrs Lewes other than with respect, said Norton, 'the women who visit her are either so éman-cipée as not to mind what the world says about them, or have no social position to maintain. Lewes dines out a good deal, and some of the men with whom he dines go without their wives to his house on Sundays.' The hostess's books must not be mentioned. Departure must be at six. Lewes, in 'his velvet coat and neat slippers', as Anthony Trollope recalled him (George Meredith described him as 'a mercurial little showman'), poured tea.

In the Leweses' circle almost everyone wrote or could write, and George Eliot and George Lewes were worth writing about. There is almost no end to their appearances in contemporary reminiscences, and opinions of them, and of the afternoons at the Priory, can be widely found in a gamut from the cruel to the adoring. Oscar Browning's is probably as neutral as any:

Mrs Lewes generally sat in an armchair at the left of the fireplace. Lewes generally stood or moved about in the back drawing-room, at the end of which was the grand piano, on which, as far as I am aware, she never played during these receptions. In the early days of my acquaintance the company was small, containing more men than women. . . . The guests closed round the fire and the conversation was general. At a later period the company increased, and those who wished to converse with the great authoress whom they had come to visit took their seat in turns at the chair by her side. She always gave us of her best. Her conversation was deeply sympathetic, but grave and solemn, illumined by happy phrases and by thrilling tenderness, but not by humour.

On a Sunday afternoon in May 1869, when the Leweses had just returned from abroad and their friends did not yet know of their arrival, only three visitors came to the Priory. These were Miss Grace Norton and Miss Sara Sedgwick with a young American friend, Henry James, brought for the first time. They were aghast to discover the household in disarray, the son Thornton, who had just returned ill from Natal, stretched in agony on the floor. Lewes was out searching for a doctor. Mrs Lewes, in black silk dress and lace mantilla, agitated and 'in no small flutter', yet managed to make polite conversation with the disconcerted visitors, telling them about the mistral in Avignon and of 'their having, on the whole scene, found pleasure further poisoned by the frequency in all those parts of "evil faces: oh the evil

Sketch of G.E. in her habitual lace mantilla. The American writer, Bret Harte, wrote of her, 'I have seldom seen a grander face. I have read some-where that she looked like a horse – a great mistake as, although her face is long and narrow, it is only as Dante's was. . . . Mrs. Lewes's eyes are grey and sympathetic, but neither large nor beautiful. Her face lights up when she smiles. . . . She reminds you continually of a man – a bright, gentle, lovable, philosophical man – without being a bit *masculine*.'

faces!"'' At last James suggested he might help by pursuing the doctor and dashed off in a four-wheeler, deeply impressed by his first contact with 'the great mind', the visit becoming invested in his mind with an aura that tinc-tured his reading of *Middlemarch*.

Thornton's illness, not then diagnosed as tuberculosis of the spine, lasted for six agonizing months. Towards the end, when hope was relinquished, Marian went out one afternoon and Agnes came for two and a half hours to sit with her son. He died on 19 October, with Marian and Nursie beside him. With ironical pathos, Lewes's replies to his friends' letters of condolence all express his thankfulness that, through Thornton's worst periods of pain and delirium, no traces of impurity appeared.

Marian had had her new novel in mind since she had published *Felix Holt*. Early in 1869 she felt ready to begin, and tried to make a start during the summer. 'Began *Middlemarch* (the Vincy and Featherstone parts)', she wrote in her Journal on 2 August, but found she could not write her novel and watch by Thornie. Instead she worked on the 'Brother and Sister' sonnets, and 'The Legend of Jubal'. After a winter of gradual, though never, for Lewes, full recovery, and the still-unfailing panacea of a journey abroad, *Middlemarch* – that is, Part II of *Middlemarch* as we now know it – slowly progressed. Then in November 1870, she laid it aside to begin a new story, 'Miss Brooke', which, it has been suggested, was a reshaping of 'The Clerical Tutor', the projected but unwritten Clerical Scene. 'It is', she wrote in her Journal, 'a subject which has been recorded among my possible themes ever since I began to write fiction.' Soon she became aware that 'Miss Brooke' could and should be an integral part of *Middlemarch*. Thenceforward the book went steadily on.

Women authors' husbands are a cross many publishers have to put up with, but Blackwood had suffered more than most, the constant recipient of jaunty, bossy letters from Lewes, instructing him how, when and where to publish and, of course, advertise. Now Lewes made the good suggestion that, instead of the usual three-decker, *Middlemarch*'s four parts should be issued as eight half-volumes to be published in instalments. The idea, though original in England, was a practical one; and once Blackwood and his colleagues had begun to read the manuscript, they would have agreed to almost anything rather than lose a novel they all instantly recognized as magnificent. The first part of *Middlemarch* was published on 1 December 1871 at 5s, the last in December 1872. In 1873 it was issued in four volumes at two guineas, then in one volume at one guinea, and in May 1874 reprinted in a one-volume edition of 10,000 copies at 7s 6d. By 1879, nearly 31,000 copies of the English and foreign editions had been sold, and Marian had made over £8,000.

Writers who need to believe that the greatest books are not recognized in their own day can find no consolation in *Middlemarch*, which was widely accepted as a masterpiece. Those who were made uneasy by it tended to suspect a Positivist thesis in the apparent limitations to each character's free will. Certainly the portraits were excellent and there was plenty of 'all the ordinary novel-reader reads a novel for'. Certainly it was noble, but in a new, strange and even melancholy way that left some reviewers uneasy. Yet, said

Dorothea Casaubon finds her husband dead in the garden (*Middlemarch*, Bk. V, Ch. xlviii); from a painting by W. L. Taylor, 1886.

the *Spectator*, speaking for most, '*Middlemarch* bids more than fair to be one of the great books of the world.'

A curiosity about *Middlemarch* is that the game of identifications, for the first time, was played not so much by the local readers but, today as then, by serious critics. The former could find Robert Evans again in Caleb Garth, Chrissey in Celia Brooke, and speculate whether Will Ladislaw, widely found unworthy of Dorothea, might be George Lewes. It was not here that critical interest has centred but on the sources for Casaubon and, to some extent, Dorothea.

Shortly before *Middlemarch* was written, the Leweses had become friendly with Mark Pattison, the Rector of Lincoln College, Oxford, and his wife Emilia, twenty-seven years younger than he, who after his death in 1884 was to marry Sir Charles Dilke; to her Marian gave what she herself admitted might be thought too great an effusiveness of 'motherly tenderness'. Some people then, as notably John Sparrow now, have found Casaubon in Mark Pattison. It may well be that Pattison's work on Isaac Casaubon, the sixteenth-century French theologian, provided the name, but the wider identification is unconvincing, and not least in the unlikelihood of George Eliot, whose recollections took so long to crystallize into fiction, making substantial use of someone so recently met. Some ten years earlier she had written to Barbara, 'my mind works with the most freedom and the keenest sense of poetry in my remote past, and there are many strata to be worked through before I can begin to use *artistically* any material I may gather in the present'. Almost to the end of her writing life, the part played by recently gathered material was trivial (and mostly geographical) as compared with that whose roots were set before she left the Midlands.

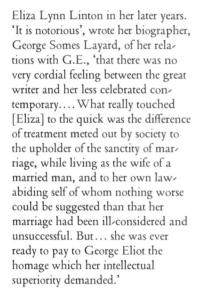

Eliza Lynn Linton in her later years. 'It is notorious', wrote her biographer, George Somes Layard, of her relations with G.E., 'that there was no very cordial feeling between the great writer and her less celebrated contemporary.... What really touched [Eliza] to the quick was the difference of treatment meted out by society to the upholder of the sanctity of marriage, while living as the wife of a married man, and to her own law-abiding self of whom nothing worse could be suggested than that her marriage had been ill-considered and unsuccessful. But... she was ever ready to pay to George Eliot the homage which her intellectual superiority demanded.'

There are other candidates for Casaubon's original. Some are literary, picked on because they portray marriages of May with December. Another real-life suggestion has been Robert Mackay, whose book had pegged Marian's first review in the *Westminster* in January 1851. G. S. Haight agrees with Eliza Lynn Linton in preferring Dr Brabant. It is true that Dr Brabant was, as Eliza put it, 'ever writing and rewriting, correcting and destroying, [but] he never got further than the introductory chapter of a book which he intended to be epoch-making and the final destroyer of superstition and theological dogma'. It certainly seems possible that Dr Brabant inspired the 'Key to all the Mythologies', but Casaubon can never have been intended for a portrait of the cocky, dapper doctor who was, said Eliza, 'always spruce and trim, and well got up and preserved'. Moreover, if this part of the story was originally intended as a Clerical Scene, it should be remarked that Brabant was not a cleric; and neither was another possibility sometimes adduced, the dryasdust German professor of Marian's post-Brabant dream. It is most probable that Casaubon was a composite. As a factor in the composition it is perhaps worth mentioning, with extreme caution, a letter from Mrs Belloc Lowndes to Elizabeth Haldane, written in 1924: 'My mother has always held the secret view that she [*sc.* George Eliot] had a passionate, illicit love affair before she ever came to London, with that very attractive man, I think a Doctor Something, with whom and with whose wife she was intimate as a girl.' If there is any basis for this statement, then the name, though unmentioned, is not beyond all conjecture.

Many originals have also been put forward for Dorothea, from literature and from life: Mrs Pattison, Mrs Mackay and, recently, Mark Pattison's sister Dora, the saintly nursing sister of Walsall. But if we read the 'Prelude' to *Middlemarch* (which Blackwood, surely wisely, would have preferred to omit) and then look in the Leweses' world for someone who could be seen as 'a Saint Theresa . . . whose loving heart-beats and sobs after an unattained goodness tremble off and are dispersed among hindrances', there can be only one answer and it is confirmed by a letter from Lewes to Blackwood: 'Surely Dorothea is the very cream of lovely womanhood. She is more like her creator than any one else and more so than any other of her creations.'

Marian accepted this identification. She thought it necessary to assure Harriet Beecher Stowe, an occasional correspondent, that Casaubon was nothing like her warm-hearted enthusiastic husband, but for some time 'Mr and Mrs Casaubon' were her and George's playful names for each other, the more suitable in that George was working doggedly on his own 'Key to all the Mythologies', a magnum opus called *Problems of Life and Mind*, uncompleted at his death. Lord Acton remarked that Ladislaw, in mocking at the 'Key', was ignorant of the state of German scholarship, and that it would have been a pioneer work; even, it has been suggested recently, forestalled *The Golden Bough*.

Middlemarch finally established George Eliot as the great secular teacher. 'In the seventies and eighties', wrote Elizabeth Haldane, 'nearly every "Mutual Improvement Society" had a lecture on "George Eliot and her moral and religious teaching",' and Gosse, 'What a solemn, what a portentous thing was the contemporary fame of George Eliot', and he recalled Herbert Spencer, on the London Library Committee, expressing strong objection to the purchase of novels, 'except, of course, those of George Eliot'.

Now the Leweses were rich. They had both known poverty, and though Blackwood's epithet 'voracious' sometimes seemed appropriate, they had several claims upon them, such as the support of Agnes and of Emily Clarke, and an annuity of £50 to old Nursie. For formal subscriptions they were not an easy touch, and where Marian's approval or sympathy was qualified, she gave only minimally. Charles Bray, appealing to her for out-of-work ribbon workers in Coventry, got only £1 with offer of another when required, and she would make such occasional contributions as two guineas to the Working Women's College in 1872. And in that year, when Elizabeth Garrett Anderson's New Hospital for Women was opened, Lewes sent an initial contribution of £5, and £2 2s annually thereafter, which Marian continued after his death, as she did the payment to Agnes.

At a Saturday morning Pop Concert in St James's Hall; sketch of G.E. by Laura Teresa Alma-Tadema, second wife of the painter Lawrence Alma-Tadema.

Both gave generously where their affections were engaged, and it is in this light that we should probably see Marian's annual £5 to the Positivist fund, since after 1878, when Frederic Harrison broke away from Richard Congreve and formed a dissident group, she gave £5 impartially to both. She gave £200 to help raise an annuity for Octavia Hill, and though Cara Bray never took her up on her constant offers of financial help, she managed in 1873 to persuade Cara to accept £50 as an advance payment for a children's story about kindness to animals. And when in 1874 she heard that her old friend and teacher Maria Lewis, now living in Leamington, was in financial straits, she sent £10 with a pleasant letter, and several times repeated the gift.

The main objects of their generosity were, naturally, the family. Lewes often gave presents to Agnes's children by Hunt, and to his widowed sister-in-law, Mrs Edward Lewes, and her son Vivian. Then there were their 'own' children and grandchildren to help and plan for. The Charles Leweses, with worrying delay after two miscarriages, at last had Blanche in 1872, Maud in 1874, and Elinor in 1877. Bertie, in Natal, married Eliza Stevenson Harrison in 1871: their daughter, born in 1872, they named Marian Lewes, and in 1875 they had a son, George Herbert. But Bertie, like Thornton, was tubercular, and in June 1875 he died at Durban. It is typical of Marian's small vulgarities that she was unable, when telling correspondents of Bertie's death, to refrain from adding that it was their comfort to be able to provide for the widow and children.

Drawing of George Henry Lewes in 1867 by Rudolph Lehmann. This artist was a brother of the wealthy industrialist Frederick Lehmann, at whose home in Highgate the Leweses met many people of distinction in the world of art and letters; and the Lehmanns were frequent visitors to the Priory.

Marian was becoming ever more conventional in her views. 'I wish there were some solid, philosophical Conservative to take the reins', she wrote during the Ministerial crisis of March 1873, and she was anxious to quash rumours that during her formally religious days she had ever adhered to any body but that of the Anglican Communion. So when the Leweses began branching out on their own account, it was in conventional ways. Marian bought an astrakhan jacket and muff, and a squirrel-lined cloak, and elegant laces for the mantillas which had become her regular indoor wear. George had a fur-lined overcoat and fancy waistcoats, and he bought some jewellery for Marian. The house received new furnishings and a new Broadwood piano. They had been hiring a brougham from a livery stable for some years, but in 1873 they bought their own carriage for £150.

In and after 1876, [wrote Gosse,] when I was in the habit of walking from the north-west of London towards Whitehall, I met several times, driven slowly homeward, a victoria which contained a strange pair in whose appearance I took a violent interest. The man, prematurely ageing, was hirsute, rugged, satyr-like, gazing vivaciously to left and right; this was George Henry Lewes. His companion was a large, thick-set sibyl, dreamy and immobile, whose massive features, somewhat grim when seen in profile were incongruously bordered by a hat, always in the height of the Paris fashion, which in those days commonly included an immense ostrich feather: this was George Eliot. The contrast between the solemnity of the face and the frivolity of the headgear had something pathetic and provincial about it.

George du Maurier's sketch of G.E. done from memory. 'Du Maurier became a favoured guest', wrote his friend Thomas Armstrong. 'He was made much of, and used to sing for them, notably his little French song, *Fi de ces vins d'Espagne*; this became a general favourite at the Priory, where it seems to me the tone must have altered very much in a few years, and that this famous salon must have become "joliment dégourdi" to call for and relish so frivolous an entertainment.'

Now, with fame and money, Marian began to acquire respectability. Mary Cash maintained, after Marian's death, that Marian had often told her that in Germany a marriage service had been performed which was valid there but not in England, and certainly rumours of some kind of private divorce and remarriage circulated widely. Under their influence, such people as Dean Stanley and his wife Lady Augusta were happy to meet George Eliot at dinner in 1871, and disconcerted, afterwards, to discover the rumours unfounded. But their circulation shows how completely Agnes remained in the background, and the Leweses, if they had not come to believe that they were somehow or other married, at least began to forget that they were not. In 1873 Lewes felt able to tell a correspondent that he had lived with his mother till he married his Dorothea.

It is a pity that Marian could not know that the Queen, who collected the Leweses' autographs and greatly admired Marian's work, did not disapprove of such liaisons as hers, 'when only, perhaps for impossibility of money, or rank, and God knows what, the outward earthly form cannot be given by man! In God's eyes, I believe, as surely as I write this, that this will be considered as holy and right' – this to her daughter in Germany in 1870. However, Marian was delighted when on two occasions she and Lewes were invited to dinner by George Goschen, the financier and Liberal politician, and his wife to meet Queen Victoria's daughters, in 1877, Princess Louise with her husband the Marquis of Lorne, and in 1878 the Crown Prince and Princess of Germany.

With respectability, the Sunday gatherings at the Priory became reverentially dull. Except when George du Maurier, Charles's neighbour in Church Row, Hampstead, came along and sang naughty French songs, 'her *réunions* had somewhat the solemnity of religious functions, with the religion cut out', said Thomas Armstrong, who in 1894 was to figure in *Trilby* as Little Billee. After Dickens's death in 1870, George Eliot was unquestionably England's greatest novelist, and her receptions now a must for respectable intellectual London. There one might see T. H. Huxley, John Tyndall, John Morley, Walter Bagehot, A. W. Kinglake, Joseph Joachim, Edward and Georgiana Burne-Jones, Robert Browning and, of course, Spencer – to name only a few regulars. But the irreverent began to stay away: '. . . the string of visitors became fatiguing to those who remembered the old days', said Oscar Browning.

For all his great talents, George Lewes had always been, in personal relationships, a vulgar and imperceptive man, and this, over the years, could not but rub off on Marian too. The role they chose for her was one of only coarse appeal, and certainly it coarsened her. One cannot but agree with Eliza Lynn Linton when she wrote,

She was a made woman – not in the French sense – but made by self-manipulation as one makes a statue or a vase. I have never known any one who seemed to me so purely artificial as George Eliot . . . never for one instant did she forget her self-created self – never did she throw away the trappings of the airs of the benign Sibyl. . . . She was so consciously 'George Eliot' – so interpenetrated head and heel, inside and out, with the sense of her importance as the great novelist and profound thinker of her generation, as to make her society a little overwhelming.

Two anecdotes of the period can show Marian at her nicest and at her most portentous, one from Oxford and one from Cambridge. The first is from Mrs Humphry Ward, in 1870 an unmarried girl of eighteen when she met the Leweses at one of Pattison's Sunday evenings at Lincoln. To George she took 'a prompt and active dislike', and George Eliot was nearly silent, 'entirely occupied in watching or listening to Mr Lewes'. But after dinner, divining young Mary Arnold's disappointment, George Eliot sat down with her outside the drawing-room, and for twenty minutes, 'with perfect ease and finish, without misplacing a word or dropping a sentence', she talked about her recent journey to Spain. 'It all comes back', wrote Mrs Ward nearly fifty years later, 'the long, pallid face, set in black lace, the evident wish to be kind to a young girl.'

The second story is from F. W. H. Myers, who walked with George Eliot in the Fellows' Garden of Trinity College, Cambridge, one rainy May evening in 1873, and she, 'taking as her text the three words . . . *God, Immortality, Duty*, – pronounced, with terrible earnestness, how inconceivable was the *first*, how unbelievable was the *second*, and yet how peremptory and absolute the *third* . . . her grave, majestic countenance turned toward me like a sibyl's in the gloom.'

It was said of a lesser Victorian novelist, Charlotte M. Yonge, that she would punish her characters by giving them what they had wanted, and in this respect Marian could have been one of Miss Yonge's characters. She received in her lifetime recognition of her genius as a novelist and of her moral stature as a teacher and finally social acceptance, but she could not always receive these gracefully. There was always, now, the tendency to mawkishness, to gushing and over-intensity. The episode of Alexander Main well illustrates the tasteless failing in sensibility that one must, in all charity, believe to have been brought out by life with Lewes.

Alexander Main was a young Scotsman who wrote an admiring letter, with a query about the pronunciation of 'Romola' in August 1871. Marian's warm acknowledgment evoked ever warmer responses, and none too warm to be welcome – 'Your last . . . made me cry. You have thoroughly understood me – you have entered with perfect insight into the significance of the poem . . . your letters have been a cup of strength to me.' Eventually, after declaring that George Eliot had been surpassed only by Shakespeare, Main asked if he could compile and publish a volume of her noble sayings. The Leweses responded enthusiastically, George coming up with the title, *Wise, Witty and Tender Sayings in Prose and Verse*, and persuading Blackwood (who privately referred to Main as 'The Gusher') to publish the book, which came out in 1871. Main followed it with *The George Eliot Birthday Book* of 1878, but by this time George, at least, had tired of his sensitivities and importunities.

As Marian grew older, her appeal to women seems even to have increased, and among the most devotedly attached to her there is usually a lack of normal emotional satisfactions. So it had been with Maria Lewis and Sara Hennell, so it was with Emilia Pattison and with Georgiana Burne-Jones, whose acquaintance with Marian turned to devotion in 1870, the time of her husband's notorious affair with Marie Zambaco. 'It is impossible to be with that noble creature without feeling *better*', Mrs Frederick Lehmann wrote in 1867 from Pau to the husband from whom she was separated by her poor health, and gradually there was established a circle of younger women whose devotion to Marian fell little short of idolatry, to whom she was 'Madonna', with the most favoured of them addressed as 'Figluola'. Among these was Elma Stuart, a young widow with an only son, living at Dinan in France.

In 1872 Elma Stuart had sent to Mrs Lewes an oak book-slide she had made and an adoring letter, followed, when this was acknowledged, by other mostly home-made gifts, photographs, and, of course, more letters. At one period the correspondence was concentrated on how best to hold up one's drawers without constriction. Marian favoured broad straps crossing at the back and attached by safety-pins. Elma urged elastic, but the Leweses, who had both tried this, found that it stretched in the wash. Elma first met the Leweses at lunch in October 1873, warned beforehand by Marian to expect to see 'a first cousin of the old Dante's – rather smoke-dried – a face with lines in it that seem a map of sorrows'. Thereafter, Marian was to be Elma's spiritual mother, and when Elma died in 1903 she was buried beside Marian in Highgate Cemetery, on her tombstone 'one whom for $8\frac{1}{2}$ blessed years George Eliot called by the sweet name of "Daughter".'

'Her great strong face (a mixture of Savonarola and Dante)', was Mary Gladstone's impression in 1878. These resemblances were often pointed out, and were not rejected. This drawing of Dante by Frederic Burton was presented by him to the Leweses in 1864.

One of many, many, usually home-made presents from Elma Stuart: 'I am at this moment writing on the really beautiful writing-board. It is not too heavy, because I rest it on the elbows of my chair, and the graining and colour, as well as the art spent on it, are soothing to my outward and inward sense.' (G.E. *Letters*, 12 January 1878.)

Edith Simcox was a more tragic admirer. The well-educated daughter of a middle-class merchant and undoubtedly an emotional lesbian ('I had always taken their [*sc.* the Leweses'] kindness as a sign that I was half a man – and they knew it', she wrote in her Autobiography), she was in all that did not relate to George Eliot an intelligent, competent woman. Especially active in the field of women's employment, she ran a shirt-makers' trade union, was a member of the London School Board, and in 1875 she and Mrs Emma Paterson, the pioneer of women's trade unionism, were the first women delegates to a Trade Union Congress. Unfortunately for her, in 1872 she fell in love with Marian who, though often impatient of Edith's devotion and obviously less drawn to her than to her other admirers, never gave her a final *congé*. Admittedly, Edith's adoration could be tiresome. One Sunday, for instance, she found the Leweses alone, and they said, well, she had better sit down, 'which I proceeded to do on the rug at her feet, which I kissed'; and on another occasion, when she did the same, she noticed that 'for the rest of the evening her feet avoided the footstool where I found them'. The Leweses had let Edith's workshop make George's shirts and Marian's underwear; but they forgot to acknowledge the book, *Natural Law*, which Edith dedicated to Marian. Still, Edith's devotion, like Elma's, never wavered until her own death in 1901, but her bare tombstone lacks the epitaph she once wrote for herself: 'Here lies the body of E.J.S., etc., whose heart's desire lives wherever the name and memory of George Eliot is beloved.'

In the autumn of 1872 the Leweses were seeking health at Homburg, and in the Rooms there Marian saw at the tables 'Miss Leigh, Byron's grand-niece, who is only 26 years old, and is completely in the grasp of this mean, money-making demon. It made me cry to see her young fresh face among the hags and brutally stupid men around her.'

'Women's Suffrage: The St. James's Hall meeting to support franchise for women house-holders was presided over by Mrs. Garrett Anderson, M.D. Other enthusiasts above are the Misses Lydia Becker, Edith Simcox. ...' (1884). Which woman is Edith Simcox is not indicated.

So *Daniel Deronda* was born. At first Marian thought the new work might become a play, but it was soon clear that here was another novel. The Jewish element of the book was integral to her conception from the start. As a young woman at Foleshill, Marian had been conventionally anti-Semitic ('almost all their history is utterly revolting. . . . Everything *specifically* Jewish is of a low grade'). But this had long since passed away, and her interest in Judaism, already apparent in her visits to old synagogues, had been fired by friendship with the renowned Talmudic scholar, Emmanuel Deutsch, who would come to the Priory to read Hebrew with Marian and to talk of his dream of a Jewish National Home in Palestine. Lewes too had a substantial contribution to make in his memories of the Philosophers' Club of working men in Red Lion Square that he used to attend in the 1840s, and of one of its members, a Jewish watchmaker called Kohn or Cohn, who had introduced him to the works of Spinoza; but the character of Mordecai Cohen was rather based on Deutsch, who died painfully of cancer in 1873.

Marian inevitably began an intensive course of reading in Jewish history and literature, and early in 1874 she was ready to begin. But in March she had to put the book aside to prepare for the press the volume of poems which was published in May, and after that, with ill-health and a constant need for

The Ludwig's Well at Bad Homburg. 'We arrive at Homburg on Saturday night. . . . The air, the waters, the plantations are all perfect—"only man is vile". I am not fond of denouncing my fellow-sinners, but gambling being a vice I have no mind to, it stirs my disgust even more than my pity.' (G.E. *Letters*, 25 September 1872.)

quiet holidays, the book slowly progressed. The Leweses were looking hard, now, for a country home in England. In 1870, with war in Europe, they had taken a furnished cottage at Shottermill near Haslemere for the early summer, and had liked it so well that, when they had to vacate it, they moved to another just across the road. It was here that Tennyson, living only a few miles away, first met Marian and read some of his poems to her. Mrs Tennyson called too, though this fact was hurriedly excised from most copies of *Alfred Lord Tennyson, a Memoir* of 1897: Tennyson later visited the Priory and in 1877 gave a poetry-reading there. Surrey had appealed and in 1872 the Leweses took another furnished house, pending finding one of their own. In the autumn of 1873 it was still a furnished house, Blackbrook near Bickley in Kent, though they hoped to buy this one, and here they were visited by Mrs Charles Darwin and went to lunch at Downe. But the purchase of Blackbrook fell through, and the right house took many years to find. In the search for it, they had the help of a new friend, John Walter Cross.

George Lewes had met the widowed Mrs William Cross at Weybridge in October 1867, when he was on a walking tour with Herbert Spencer. Mrs Cross was in Rome in the spring of 1869, and called on the Leweses there with her younger son John, then twenty-nine years old, a broker who had been working in New York and was now about to enter his firm's London office. All the family, including the son-in-law, William Bullock-Hall, of Six Mile Bottom near Cambridge (his wife died just before Thornie), became great friends of the Leweses, and John quickly became not only Johnny but an adoptive nephew, receiving letters from Marian signed 'Your affectionate Aunt'. To Johnny, Lewes entrusted the family investments, and enthusiastically Johnny took up the search for the country-house.

Marian's health was especially poor around this time. She had been troubled with painful neuralgia for some years, and to this was added, early in 1874, a bad attack of the kidney stone from which her father had died, and which troubled her intermittently thereafter. Lewes, for the time being the stronger of the two, nursed her devotedly through it, but throughout the seventies her letters reveal an obsession with the approach of death, and especially with the fear, which was to be realized, that Lewes would die first.

Marian was still struggling with *Daniel Deronda* – originally 'Daniel de Ronda' and pronounced by Lewes Dĕ Rōnda – when in 1875 they took a house for the summer at Rickmansworth. Blackwood had offered the same terms as for *Middlemarch*, 2s for each 5s part sold, and a royalty of 40 per cent. Though Marian did not complete the story until 8 June 1876, the first of the eight parts was issued on 1 February of that year and the last in September, with the four bound volumes out in August.

Jewish readers were especially delighted with the book, and several claimed to recognize themselves or their friends in Daniel. The author received an appreciative letter from the Ashkenazi Chief Rabbi, Dr Hermann Adler, and an appreciative review in the *Gentleman's Magazine* from the Sephardic historian James Picciotto, though he pointed out some trifling errors in Jewish practices. Non-Jewish professional reviewers tended, then as now, to be of the opinion that in *Daniel Deronda* George Eliot had imperfectly

The old synagogue at Frankfurt, c. 1850. '–to Frankfurt where we stayed 5 days in order that we might attend service at the Synagogue (for Mutter's purposes)' G.H.L. to Charles, 9 August 1873). 'It was on this journey that [Deronda] first entered a Jewish Synagogue – at Frankfort,' (*Daniel Deronda*, Bk. IV, Ch. xxxii.)

The first page of the manuscript of *Daniel Deronda*.

Chapter I.

3

Men can do nothing without the make-believe of a beginning. Even Science, the strict measurer, is obliged to start with a make-believe unit, & must fix on a point in the stars' unceasing journey when his sidereal clock shall pretend that time is at Naught: his less accurate Grandmother Poetry has always been understood to start in the middle; but on reflexion it appears that her proceeding is not very different from his; since Science too reckons backwards as well as forwards, divides his unit into billions, & with his clock-finger at Naught really sets off in medias res. No retrospect will take us to the true beginning; & whether our prologue be in heaven or on earth, it is but a fraction of that all-presupposing fact with which our story sets out.

Was she beautiful or not beautiful? and what was the secret of form or expression which gave the dynamic quality to her glance & made it an epoch? Was the good or the evil genius dominant in those beams? Probably the evil; else why was the effect that of unrest rather than of undisturbed charm? Why was the wish to look again felt as coercion & not as a longing in which the whole being consents?

She who raised these questions in Daniel Deronda's mind was occupied in gambling: not in the open air under a Southern sky, tossing coppers on a ruined wall with rags about her limbs; but in one of those splendid resorts which the enlightenment of ages has prepared for the same species of pleasure at a heavy cost of gilt mouldings, dark-toned colour & chubby nudities, all correspondingly heavy – forming a suitable condenser for human breath, belonging in great part to the highest

'–full-length portraits with deep backgrounds, inserted in the cedar panelling–surmounted by a ceiling that glowed with the rich colours of the coats of arms ranged between the sockets–'. Is Sir Hugo Mallinger's drawing-room at Topping Abbey (*Daniel Deronda*, Bk. V, Ch. xxxv) an echo of the panelled room at Maxstoke Priory, whose ceiling is seen above?

combined two separate tales; of these, most found the Jewish story senti-mental and tiresome, while respecting and admiring that part of the story sometimes called 'Gwendolen Harleth'. But a few critics were already pre-pared to consider the book as a unified whole, and to see it, with all its faults, as a grander achievement and greater potential than anything George Eliot had yet done. The most lastingly famous review was by Henry James, a conversation between Pulcheria, Theodora and Constantinius, published in the *Atlantic Monthly* of December 1876. Constantinius takes the curate's-egg view, finding, despite excellences, a consistent 'want of tact', a presenta-tion of 'views upon life' instead of 'feeling life itself'. Theodora, who is enthusiastic for the book, says it is 'a complete world . . . so vast, so much-embracing'. Pulcheria finally dismisses it as 'a very awkward and ill-made story' about 'A silly young girl and a heavy, overwise young man who *don't* fall in love with her!'

Though there may still be elements from Marian's early life in *Daniel Deronda*, in this book it is clear that she has at last worked through those strata of her remote past of which she wrote to Barbara, and is now not only able to make easy use of recently garnered material but to integrate it so well that few identifications can be more than partial. Mordecai, undoubtedly, is based on Deutsch, and Klesmer almost certainly on the composer and pianist Anton Rubinstein (a first cousin four times removed of the present writer), whom the Leweses had first met in Weimar in 1854 and met again in London in May 1876. In Mirah Lapidoth some people saw Barbara Bodichon's pro-tégée Phoebe (or 'Hertha') Marks, who would sing Hebrew songs to Marian and Barbara. But Marian was well into the book before she met Phoebe, and the account of Mirah's drawing-room début recalls that of Sally Shilton as told in Lady Newdigate's letters; the child Mary Ann could have heard of it in the Arbury housekeeper's room, or, indeed, from Sally herself. Sir Hugo Mallinger's Topping Abbey is widely said to be based on Lacock Abbey, which the Leweses had visited in 1874; but the reference to the 'northern cloister' may imply some link with the not dissimilar cloisters of *Adam Bede*; there are foliated pillars, as required, at Croxden Abbey. Moreover, at Maxstoke Priory near Fillongley, where Marian's Aunt Garner and Uncle Isaac Pearson lived, there is, according to the local guide, 'a remarkable panelled room with a painted ceiling showing the crests of many families', just as in Sir Hugo's drawing-room. The distinctive stables in the old chapel have not found an original. It might be worth considering again Calwich Abbey; a *History and Topography* of the neighbourhood of 1839 writes of Calwich, 'The ancient Hermitage has been converted into stables, but some portions of the original fabric yet remain. The north wall, with pointed gables, is nearly entire.'

In Gwendolen's guilty belief that she could have saved Grandcourt from drowning, some people have seen a close resemblance to a story by Paul Heyse published in 1858, the year in which Marian met Heyse in Munich. In it, a Neapolitan fisherman's moment of hesitation denies him the chance of saving a drowning friend. And one episode in the book, Mirah's intended suicide, provides a type example of the way Marian had, as so often, in earlier books, changed only the superficialities of reality and then been outraged when readers presumed to identify the core. This episode is undoubtedly based on Mary Wollstonecraft's attempted suicide in 1795; Marian had been writing of this to Deutsch in 1872 and of the 'real joys' which could follow such despair. But where Mary had deliberately wetted her garments in the rain so as to sink the easier, and then jumped from Putney Bridge, Mirah wetted her cloak from the bank, and the place of her attempt was by Kew Bridge.

In the autumn of 1876 Johnny Cross at last found the right country-house for the Leweses, the Heights at Witley near Haslemere, a large red-brick in some eight acres of ground which they secured for £4,950. But it needed much alteration, and they were not able to move in until June 1877, sending the servants down a few days before. Since 1871, when Grace and Amelia had left them after ten years' service, Marian had been lucky in her staff. Rufa Call, who was going to Italy, had passed on an excellent cook-housekeeper, Mrs Mary Dowling, and two maids, Elizabeth and Charlotte, to whom was later added a parlourmaid, Brett. These could be safely trusted to look after one or other home when the Leweses were away, and to manage such entertaining as was called for.

At the Heights the Leweses did not entertain much, though they occasionally had friends to stay. Blackwood had never succeeded in persuading Marian to his own passion, golf, though he had made her try one day at Blackheath and she showed, he told her, talent. Now Johnny Cross, a devoted player of both 'real' and the new lawn tennis, persuaded the Leweses to take up the latter. But Lewes was too ill now for much activity, though through 1877 and early 1878 the routine of their lives continued. When in London they still went, as they had for many years, to the weekly Popular Concerts on Saturday afternoons at St James's Hall. It was known that this was the one public place where George Eliot could be seen, and many people went there simply to see her, or sometimes to touch her dress as she passed, or sometimes to snatch a sketch – Lowes Dickinson, Mrs Alma-Tadema and Princess Louise among them. Mrs W. K. Clifford described the Leweses at the concert hall, 'He happy and alert . . . she in black or soft grey, with a lace veil hanging in front of her bonnet, or thrown back and making a sort of halo round her head.' Lucy Clifford was a visitor to the Priory, and one of the people who liked Lewes – 'his expression was so pleasant, so kindly . . . he made one think of a dog in many ways – a rather small, active, very intelligent dog.'

At Whitsun 1878, they paid what since 1873 had been an annual visit to Benjamin Jowett at Balliol, and in October they went to Six Mile Bottom where Henry Bullock-Hall had remarried. Among the party they found there was Turgenev, whom Lewes had first met in 1859, and who became a frequent visitor to the Priory. At dinner Lewes proposed a toast to him as 'the greatest living novelist' and Turgenev transferred the toast to George Eliot. At this party Oscar Browning met the Leweses for the last time.

It was at the Heights that Henry James paid his last visit. He was staying near by with garrulous feather-headed Mrs Richard Greville, and on 1

George Eliot sketched by Princess Louise on her programme, at a concert for the Music School of the Blind, in 1877. G. S. Haight quotes a–then–young lady who saw G.E. at a concert and wondered 'why genius was so terribly homely. George Eliot wore a monstrous cross between a hat and a cap, and her dress was not beautiful; but her face lighted up wonderfully when she spoke.'

'We went with Johnnie to Witley to see a house.... Enchanted with the house and grounds. The day transcendently beautiful made everything look glorious.' (G.H.L. *Diary*, 29 November 1876.) The Heights at Witley, now an old people's home.

November 1878, a day of torrential rain, she decided they should call on the Leweses; to whom, a fortnight before, she had lent a copy of James's new novel, *The Europeans*. James told himself doubtfully that 'given the dreadful drenching afternoon we were after all an imaginable short solace'. But 'I see again our bland, benign, commiserating hostess beside the fire in a chill desert of a room . . . and I catch once more the impression of . . . their liking us to have come, mainly from a prevision of how they should more devoutly like it when we departed.' Tea was not offered, and the obviously unwanted callers were retiring to the carriage when Lewes hurried towards them with a pair of blue-bound volumes, crying, 'Ah, those books – take them away, please, away, away!', those books being 'the uninvited, the verily importunate loan' of *The Europeans*.

Haight comments that James, in his bruised disappointment that George Eliot, 'sitting in that queer bleak way . . . [in] the center of such a circle of gorgeous creation', wouldn't accept him as doing 'her sort of work', failed to sense what he calls 'the tragic misery on that sad hearthstone'. Lewes was

108

ill, suffering, as he thought, from piles. He and Marian struggled to Brighton for a few days to see Emily Clarke, then returned to the Priory and consulted their doctor, Sir James Paget, who diagnosed 'a thickening of the mucous membrane'. The pain was often intense. By 29 November it was clear that Lewes was dying, and Johnny Cross left his mother's deathbed to support Marian and Charles Lewes. On 30 November George Lewes died. On 3 December he was buried at Highgate Cemetery, with Unitarian rites conducted by Dr Thomas Sadler. Marian did not go. For 1 January 1879, her only diary entry is 'Here I and sorrow sit.'

Edith Simcox had called daily but did not venture to be asked in. She rendered Marian a service in persuading the maid Brett, who had been recounting tales of her mistress's uncontrolled screams, to be more discreet. Charles was all and more than any true son could have been, coping with letters of condolence – there was one from Isaac's wife – dealing, with Cross's

George Henry Lewes's tombstone in Highgate Cemetery. 'We had 24 years of constantly growing love, and I have this comfort–the belief that he never knew he was dying–never felt that we were parting.' (G.E. to Cara Bray, 1 April 1879.)

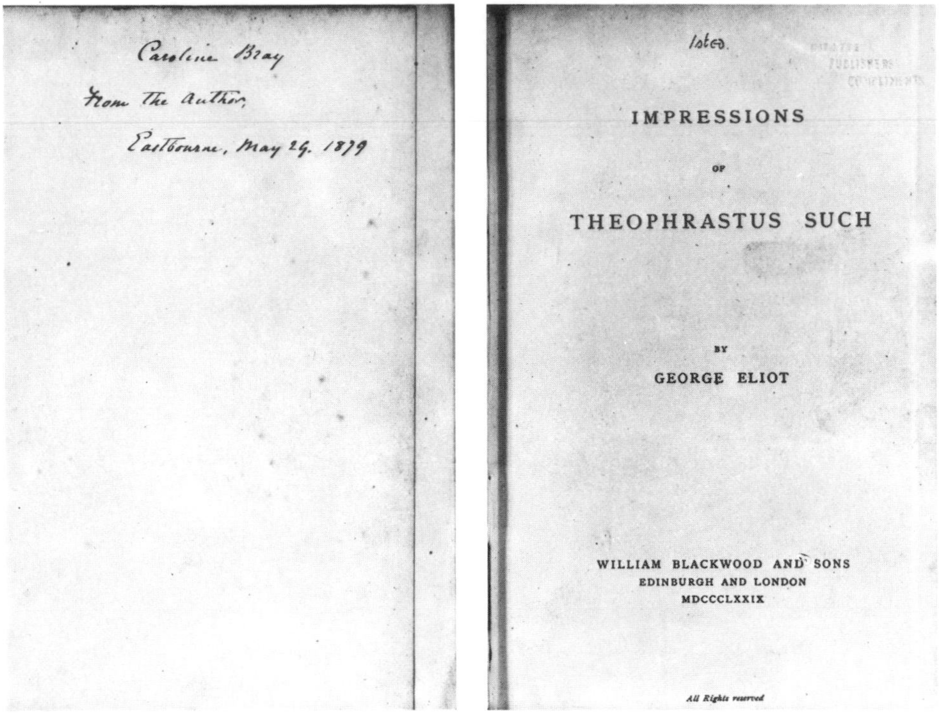

Caroline Bray
from The author,
Eastbourne, May 29. 1879

IMPRESSIONS

OF

THEOPHRASTUS SUCH

BY

GEORGE ELIOT

WILLIAM BLACKWOOD AND SONS
EDINBURGH AND LONDON
MDCCCLXXIX

All Rights reserved

The copy of *Theophrastus Such* that Marian inscribed for Cara Bray. The only other copies she gave were to Charles, to Maria Congreve, and to Sir James Paget, her doctor. 'I do not like to make presents of my own books', she wrote to Blackwood on 20 May 1879. 'It was always my Husband who desired them to be sent.'

help, with necessary business, leaving Marian in peace to choose, as he put it, 'her own way and her own time of struggling back to life'. After a week alone in her room, she came down to work on George's unfinished book, *Problems of Life and Mind.* On 7 January she wrote her first letter, to Barbara Bodichon, and soon turned to a task she liked to think would have pleased George, the completion of her own book of clubman-like essays, *Impressions of Theophrastus Such*, though worried, as she told Blackwood, lest the public should think she had been working on her own book since her husband's death when in fact she had been principally occupied with *his* manuscripts. But Blackwood encouraged her, believing that the taking up again of normal life through work would be the best thing for her. 'She is evidently getting on all right', he wrote to his nephew Willie Blackwood, 'and will soon I hope shake off the pretended sympathisers who encourage morbid notions about poor Lewes' memory.'

By early February Marian was able to go for a drive, and two weeks later she saw Johnny Cross for the first time. The faithful Edith was not let in until April, though Marian had already felt able to receive Maria Congreve, Georgie Burne-Jones, Elma Stuart and Spencer. *Theophrastus Such* was published in May. It was only politely received.

Of great help in recalling Marian to life was her decision to found in Lewes's name a Studentship in Physiology at Cambridge. To achieve this, it was necessary to have discussions with such people as Henry Sidgwick and Dr Michael Foster, and to deal with her business affairs. Lewes's simple will, written in a few lines at Wandsworth in 1859, had left his copyrights to his three sons (only Charles surviving to inherit), and the rest of his property to 'Mary Ann Evans, Spinster'. (This, when published, outraged Fanny Houghton: 'her name ought not to have been mentioned'.) All Marian's property was in Lewes's name. Charles made a formal and pathetic Declaration stating that the earnings these monies represented were not in fact his father's but Marian's. They were transferred to her as Mary Ann Evans, and retransferred when she took, by deed-poll, the added name of Lewes – why had she not done this sooner? Lewes's own estate was valued at under £2,000. The George Henry Lewes Studentship, available to either sex, was established with a capital of £5,000, the first student being a Dr C. S. Roy; Sir Charles Sherrington was to be one of several distinguished George Henry Lewes Students.

Soon other more trying demands were being made on Marian, of a kind that Lewes had hitherto dealt with. Lewes's nephew Vivian thought he might need financial help. Bessie Belloc asked for a loan of £500. Bertie's widow Eliza, who had been living with her children in Natal on an allowance from the Leweses, now brought them to England, where they arrived in April, Eliza hoping to be asked to make her home at the Priory, noisily disappointed when she was not. More and more Marian came to rely on Johnny Cross as her support. Edith Simcox had half hoped it might be she, but when on a visit in early 1880 she 'murmured broken words of love', Marian forced herself to say expressly what, to Edith's distress, she had often implied, 'that the love of men and women for each other must always be more and better than any other and bade me not wish to be wiser than "God who made me" . . . Then she said – perhaps it would shock me – she had never all her life cared very much for women . . . the friendship and intimacy of men was more to her.' Though Edith could not yet know it, it was already far too late for any woman to fill Lewes's place.

In the autumn of 1879 there came another loss. On 29 October good sensible honourable John Blackwood died. He had always seen Marian clearly, seen her whole, known her to be sometimes untruthful, sometimes gushingly silly, and yet 'a noble creature'. 'I suppose I am about the oldest and truest [friend] she has,' he had written when Lewes died, and her truest, most disinterested friend he had been.

But Marian was armoured now against loss. She had spent the summer at Witley, sustained by Johnny Cross. They had affection and some memories in common. It is hard to see what else except bereavement. He had lost a mother, she a husband.

They read the *Divinia Commedia* together. By August they were in love. From October, a passionate love-letter from her to him survives: 'Best loved and loving one', it begins, '– the sun it shines so cold, so cold, when there are no eyes to look love on me', and it is signed, 'thy tender Beatrice.'

True, she was not fitted to stand alone, must depend on the arm of man. But it was astonishingly quick, especially for a fearfully conventional Victorian widow whose first year of mourning was not yet up; the love-letter quoted above was written on mourning writing-paper. It was so quick, so short a time after the Little Man's death that it demands, sadly, consideration of a possibility that Eliza Lynn Linton draws attention to by the common device of denying it, that 'in her moment of deepest grief she had discovered proofs of Lewes's infidelity'.

Unfortunately there are, as with so many of Eliza's innuendoes, supporting indications; it would be going too far to call them evidence. After Lewes's death Marian spent much time going through his Journals and other papers. Until the middle of April 1879 her references to him in her letters are solemnly reverential. After that they appear only in a businesslike way and where necessary. Possibly relevant is that on 3 May she asks, unprecedentedly and for the only time, that Edward Burne-Jones shall spare her half an hour. On 16 May the single word 'Crisis' appears in her Diary. On 19 May, to the section on remorse in Part IV of Lewes's *Problems of Life and Mind* (it was published separately as *The Study of Psychology*), she added five lines from Wordsworth's *The Excursion* (iii. 850–5) which included,

> *The Wife and Mother pitifully fixing*
> *Tender reproaches, insupportable!*

(In this context the whole passage from line 844 seems pregnant.) Finally, this miserable supposition would clarify an otherwise enigmatic passage in Oscar Browning's *Life*, where he wrote:

A remarkable feature in Romola's character . . . corresponds to something which George Eliot probably found in her own nature. It is the suddenness with which her passionate love turns to loathing when she discovers that Tito has been false to her.

This can hardly apply to any man in Marian's life except Lewes. Marian's love for Lewes certainly did not turn to loathing at any time between the mid-1860s, when Browning first met the couple, and Lewes's death. But as a knowledgeable reference to a post-mortem discovery of infidelity, the passage makes sense.

Johnny had been asking Marian to marry him. Twice she refused because the age gap of over twenty years seemed too great. But surely she recalled that in 1877, when Thackeray's daughter Annie married Richmond Ritchie, nearly twenty years younger, she herself had written to Barbara that she had known several instances of 'young men with even brilliant advantages' choosing 'as their life's companion a woman whose attractions are wholly of the spiritual order'. On 9 April 1880 Marian consulted her doctor. On his advice, that same day she accepted Johnny's third proposal. Johnny broke the news to Charles who was delighted and, surely, relieved.

A trousseau was bought, and a house, No. 4 Cheyne Walk, Chelsea. Settlements were drawn up. Usually the group to which Marian belonged chose Unitarian rites where rites were appropriate; for marriage a registrar's office was also available. Marian chose neither. On 6 May 1880, Mary Ann Lewes, as she now truly was, married John Walter Cross at St George's, Hanover Square, the bride being given away by Charles Lee Lewes. After a night at the Lord Warden Hotel in Dover, the couple proceeded to Venice for their honeymoon.

(*Opposite*) '*Saturday 10 April 1880* To Chelsea to look at No. 4 Cheyne Walk.' (G.E.'s *Diary*.)

Marian had herself written to tell the news to a few close friends such as Barbara and Cara, who were both glad she should have a renewed chance of happiness. She left to Charles the more difficult task of telling the devotees. Their reactions were mixed. Maria Congreve was deeply hurt, Georgie Burne-Jones uneasy. Edith was pained and 'fought off the tears. If I ever write another book I shall dedicate it to the loved memory of George Henry Lewes', she wrote after Charles had gone. (Typically, Marian's excuse for not telling friends herself beforehand was that there was only a fortnight between the decision and the ceremony. In fact there was a month; Marian and Johnny were looking at the new house together the day after she accepted him.) Outsiders were not on the whole sympathetic, though few so harsh as Eliza, who said that George Eliot's second marriage 'stultified and degraded her past, and took from it that softening veil of poetry and quasi-sanctity which intense passion and unswerving constancy would have given it to the end'. More sensibly, Annie Thackeray Ritchie shocked Charles by saying that this was bound to affect George Eliot's influence, 'but it was better to be genuine than to have influence, and that I didn't suppose she imagined herself inspired, though her clique did'. On 17 May Isaac broke the silence of twenty-three years with a letter of congratulations to his sister, hoping that 'the happy event' would afford her 'much happiness and comfort'.

But all was not well at Venice. Marian, as usual, had wonderfully recovered health and spirits as soon as the Channel was crossed, and the long en-route letters to families and friends are rapturous; to Cross's sister, Marian wrote from Milan that their life had been 'a chapter of delights'. But in Venice, Johnny jumped from the balcony of their hotel room into the Grand Canal. He was pulled out by gondoliers, given chloral to calm him, and Marian desperately telegraphed for his elder brother Willie. They nursed him together and he soon recovered and was able to continue the wedding journey through Austria and Germany. There was talk of an acute mental derangement, but throughout his long life – he died in 1924 aged eighty-four – nothing of the kind occurred again.

The summer of 1880 was spent at Witley, with visiting and entertaining, with tennis and, on wet days, shuttlecock. In August, they stayed with the Bullock-Halls. The party included Lady Jebb, who wrote, 'George Eliot, old as she is, and ugly, really looked very sweet and winning in spite of both . . . she made me feel sad for her. There was not a person in the drawing-room, Mr Cross included, whose mother she might not have been. . . . He may forget the twenty years' difference between them, but she never can.'

That difference was not to irk her for long. In September Marian once again fell ill with kidney infection, and neither treatment nor a brief holiday at Brighton put her completely right. At the end of November they left Witley and, after spending a few days in an hotel, were able to move into the new house on 4 December. On 17 December they went to St George's Hall for a performance by Oxford undergraduates of *Agamemnon* in Greek, and decided afterwards that they must read the Greek dramatists together. The next day Edmund Gosse sat behind them on their usual visit to the Saturday Pop Concert, and noticed Mrs Cross, in evident discomfort,

Isaac Pearson Evans (1816–90).

– were another childhood world my share,
I would be born a little sister there.

(The last lines of *Brother and Sister*.)

tightening a white wool shawl round her shoulders. That evening she played over some of the music they had heard. The next day, Sunday, 19 December, Herbert Spencer called, and later Edith Simcox, who noticed that Marian had a sore throat. During the night it got worse and, though no danger was then feared, her kidney affliction struck her again. By Wednesday she had collapsed. 'Tell them I have great pain in the left side', she whispered to Johnny, and then she became unconscious, and died at ten o'clock that night, 22 December 1880.

There was some talk of interment in the Abbey, but it was not pursued, and on 29 December she was buried with Unitarian rites beside George Lewes in Highgate Cemetery. Among the mourners Oscar Browning noticed an elderly man, 'tall and slightly bent, his features recalling with a striking veracity the lineaments of the dead' – Isaac Evans. 'O may I join the choir invisible', was sung at the graveside.

George Eliot's grave in unconsecrated ground at Highgate Cemetery, with Elma Stuart's beside it.

Marian had signed a new will immediately after the wedding ceremony. Including her marriage settlement from Cross, she left just under £43,000. It was presumably with Cross's agreement that she left him nothing; nor were any mementoes left to family or to friends. Emily Clarke received £5,000, Vivian Lewes, George's nephew, £1,000, and £12,500 was left in trust for Bertie's widow and children. There were annuities of £40 for Mrs Dowling, the housekeeper, and of £100 for Cara Bray who was to die in 1905. Everything else went to Charles, who was the sole executor.

'I am left alone in this new House we meant to be so happy in', Cross wrote in his desolation the day after Marian's death, and Charles was glad to consent to Cross's use of George and Marian's papers, which he worked on according to his own theory of the art of biography:

I do not know that the particular method in which I have treated the letters has ever been adopted before. Each letter has been pruned of everything that seemed to me irrelevant to my purpose – of everything I thought my wife would have wished to be omitted.

'Everything' could hardly exclude Mr Lewes. It could and did exclude Chapman, and this episode, though widely known among contemporaries, was not brought to public light until the 1930s. The Venice disaster was so well camouflaged as an intestinal complaint that as late as 1955, when Haight completed his edition of George Eliot's letters, he concluded that Walter Sichel's account of the incident was 'vulgar, malicious gossip'; and only by 1968, for his biography, had he discovered that this was the true version.

Cross's *Life of George Eliot* was published in 1882. It was disastrous to George Eliot, for in attempting to conceal not merely possible scandal but the smallest flaw, he presented only a whited sepulchre; and it is impossible to feel confident that all the whitewash has yet been removed. This hagio-latrous biography was more than contemporaries could stomach, and George Eliot's literary reputation, till then almost supreme, almost immediately slumped. In 1902 W. C. Brownell's deservedly forgotten *George Eliot* could fairly open, 'How long is it since George Eliot's name has been the subject of even a literary allusion? What has become of a vogue that only yesterday, it seems, was so great?', and in the same year Arthur Machen in *Hieroglyphics*, a study of the novel, contemptuously dismissed her as 'poor, dreary, draggle-tailed George Eliot'.

It was in France that interest first revived, when in 1912 the critic V. G. M. De Vogüé named George Eliot, with Thackeray and Dickens, as the culmi-nation of an English tradition of literary realism that began with Richardson. But we do not take our literary fashions from France, and it was not until 1919 that English curiosity was rewhetted by Virginia Woolf's assessment of *Middlemarch* as 'the magnificent book which with all its imperfections is one of the few English novels written for grown-up people'. Still interest grew only slowly, and George Eliot's proper reinstatement in English literature had to wait until 1948 for F. R. Leavis's essay in *The Great Tradition* and Joan Bennett's *George Eliot: Her Mind and her Art*. Since then the flow of critical assessment has never ebbed; though full account has not yet been taken of that aspect of her work that so much impressed her contemporaries and enabled her to retain educated working-class respect after the intelligentsia had dropped her – her moral teaching.

Nothing but fashion can now detract from George Eliot's genius. For Mary Ann Evans, George Eliot's plea for Maggie Tulliver will do – 'a character essentially noble but liable to great error – error that is anguish to its own nobleness'.

A NOTE ON THE NEWDIGATES AND DAVENPORTS

In the early part of the eighteenth century, three important properties were carved out of the one-time Fleetwood estates at Ellastone, Staffordshire. On one stood Wootton Lodge, until recently occupied by the Unwin family. Another part of the estate, the ruinous Augustinian Abbey of Calwich, had been bought in 1734 by Bernard Granville, who built another house beside it; like Sir Roger Newdigate, Bernard Granville, who died in 1775, passed over the nephew he had treated as his heir and brought in a younger brother. The third portion of the estate had been bought by Richard Davenport of Calveley, Cheshire, and on it he built a stone mansion, Wootton Hall. It was he who let it to Rousseau in 1766–67.

Richard Davenport had no sons. He married his daughter Bridget to John Bromley of Baginton, Warwickshire, and his daughter Phoebe to her cousin Davies Davenport of Capesthorne Hall, Cheshire, the principal family seat. Davies's and Phoebe's son married Charlotte, daughter of Ralph Sneyd of Keele Hall, and Charlotte's sister Frances married Francis Parker, later Parker-Newdigate – Francis I. Francis I rented Wootton Hall from the Davenports of Capesthorne from, probably, 1783 to 1804.

Francis I was always on good terms with Sir Roger Newdigate, he and his wife being known affectionately at Arbury as the Little Man (as George Eliot was later to refer to Lewes) and the Little Woman, a relationship apparently unaffected by Sir Roger's virtual disinheritance of Francis II in favour of Charles Parker and his descendants.

It is possible that when Sir Roger Newdigate inherited from his brother in 1734, the property was entailed; for what it is worth, George Eliot says that it was in 'Mr Gilfil's Love Story'. She further says that Sir Christopher Cheverel (i.e. Sir Roger) went to great pains to break the entail, and, if the estate had been entailed, this is what Sir Roger must have done. It has not been possible to discover if an entail did exist, but it is the present writer's guess that Captain Wybrow is based not on Charles I but on Francis II, and that it was the latter's behaviour to Sally Shilton that led to the estate's being left away from him.

The later years of Francis I's tenure of Arbury, from 1824 to 1834, were partly occupied with Bills in Chancery brought against him by the next heirs, who claimed that he had cut and sold for his own profit timber not due to him as tenant only for life. This business must have been continuously troublesome to Robert Evans, since the timber would have been in his charge.

Francis II remains a shadowy figure. In 1808 his father repaired the partly ruined Astley Castle for him. He was living there in 1820 when he married Lady Barbara Legge, by whom he had eight sons, but soon after that the Castle was let to Lord Lifford, often named as being among Robert Evans's employers. On Francis I's death in 1835, Francis II inherited the Kirk Hallam property. In 1859, when he was a Lieutenant-Colonel in the Coldstream Guards, George Eliot refers to him as living at Blackheath, and comments, rightly, that he was a nearer relation to Sir Roger than the present holder of Arbury. He died in 1862 at Byrkley Lodge, Sneyd family property near Burton-on-Trent, where Maria Edgworth, also related to the Sneyds, used often to stay. One of his sons was then Rector of West Hallam, one was Vicar of Kirk Hallam, and his eldest son Francis William inherited the Kirk Hallam property. This eldest son must have died before 1887, for in that year, when Charles Newdigate-Newdegate died unmarried, it was another son of Francis II's, Edward, who inherited Arbury and, as Sir Roger had requested, added the older Newdegate to his name.

On the death of Richard Davenport's daughter, Bridget Bromley, in 1822, both the Bromley property at Baginton and Wootton Hall passed to a younger son of the Davenports of Capesthorne, the Reverend Walter Davenport, who thereupon added Bromley to his name. Baginton, Wootton and Capesthorne were joined under one owner in 1867, under William Davenport Bromley, who changed the name in 1868 to its present form of Bromley-Davenport. He, like the Reverend Walter, was a good landlord, and the Evans family at Ellastone benefited from his tenure.

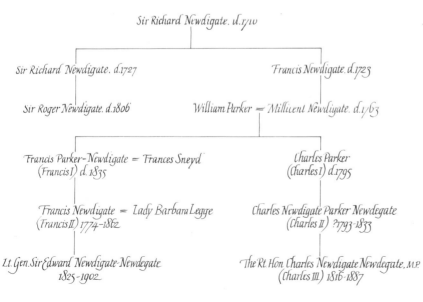

A simplified Newdigate pedigree

LIST OF ILLUSTRATIONS

logy by George Combe, 5th edition, volume I, 1843.

George Eliot; study in pencil by Caroline Bray, c. 1842. Original in the possession of W. H. Draper. Photo Radio Times Hulton Picture Library.

28 Charles Hennell; watercolour, possibly by Caroline Bray, c. 1833. Coventry City Libraries.

29 George Eliot, watercolour by Caroline Bray, 1842. National Portrait Gallery, London.

30 Statuette of Christ; plaster cast of Thorvaldsen's statue. Photo Eileen Tweedy.

Print of the head of Christ; given by George Eliot to John Sibree. Coventry City Libraries. Photo Eileen Tweedy.

31 George Eliot; outline drawn from shadow and detail filled in later by Sara Hennell, c. 1846. Photo Radio Times Hulton Picture Library.

George Eliot's copy of Thomas à Kempis's *De Imitatione Christi*; Signed 'Mary Ann Evans, February 1849, to Sara S. Hennell, January 1851'. Coventry City Libraries.

32 Robert Evans's tomb, Chilvers Coton churchyard. Photo Eileen Tweedy.

33 Part of the will of Aunt Evarard of Attleborough. Photograph of Crown Copyright Probate Records in the Lichfield Joint Record Office appear by permission of the Controller of the Stationery Office. Photo J. E. Rackham.

Aunt Evarard of Attleborough. Property of Robert S. Winser.

Photo by courtesy of Mrs Michael Womersley.

35 François D'Albert-Durade; self-portrait in watercolour. Bibliothèque Publique et Universitaire, Geneva. Photo Albert Grivel, Geneva.

George Eliot; painting by François D'Albert-Durade. National Portrait Gallery, London.

The Campagne Plongeon, Geneva; lithograph. Bibliothèque Publique et Universitaire, Geneva. Photo Albert Grivel, Geneva.

36 Dr John Chapman; oil on canvas, by John Joseph Benjamin Constant, c. 1885. Nottingham Museum and Art Gallery. Photo Layland Ross.

37 Rosehill; interior showing Elizabeth Rebecca Hennell; watercolour by Sara Hennell. Coventry City Libraries. Photo Eileen Tweedy.

38 Kenilworth Castle; watercolour by Sara Hennell, 1836. Coventry City Libraries. Photo Eileen Tweedy.

39 Bessie Parkes, c. 1860. From *Marian Evans and George Eliot* by Lawrence and Elisabeth Hanson, Oxford University Press, 1952.

40 Herbert Spencer at the age of thirty-eight. Coventry City Libraries. Photo Eileen Tweedy.

41 Kew Gardens, from *The Stationer's Almanack*, 1854; engraved by H. Adland, drawn by W. Lacey. British Museum, Department of Prints and Drawings.

42 George Henry Lewes; pencil drawing by Anne Gliddon, 1840.

National Portrait Gallery, London.

43 Agnes Lewes, G. H. Lewes and Thornton Leigh Hunt; pencil sketch by W. M. Thackeray. National Portrait Gallery, London.

45 View of Weimar, c. 1840–50; lithograph. Staatsbibliothek, Berlin.

46 St Ann's Well, Malvern; lithograph by J. Bradley, printed by C. Hullmandel. British Museum, Department of Prints and Drawings. Photo Eileen Tweedy.

47 Sara Hennell and Caroline Bray; daguerreotypes, c. 1850. Coventry City Libraries.

48 Goethe's house, Weimar. Schiller Museum, Marbach.

49 Berlin: the Pariser Platz, c. 1840; lithograph. Staatsbibliothek, Berlin.

50 Detail of the 'Balloon map' of London as seen from the north; published by Appleyard and Hetling, London 1851, and executed for the Great Exhibition. British Museum, Map Department. Photo Eileen Tweedy.

51 Part of a letter from 'Marian' to Sara Hennell, Richmond, 8 November 1856. Coventry City Libraries. Photo Eileen Tweedy.

52 Dr Eugène Bodichon; from a photograph by Mr Valentine Leigh Smith. From *Barbara Bodichon 1827–1891*, by Hester Burton, John Murray, 1949.

53 George Henry Lewes's *Sea-Side Studies*, 1858; frontispiece and title-page. Coventry City Libraries. Photo Eileen Tweedy.

79 A scene from *Silas Marner*; watercolour by Oliver Madox Brown, exhibited 1872. City of Manchester Art Galleries.

80 View of Florence, after the drawing by J.D. Harding. Engraving by James Redaway, published 1846. Photo Radio Times Hulton Picture Library.

82 *Romola looking after the poor*, by Sir Frederic Leighton. Illustration to *Romola* in the de luxe Limited Edition, 1880. Photo Mansell Collection.

Barbara Leigh-Smith in the pursuit of Art, unconscious of small humanity; from *Barbara Bodichon, 1827–1891*, by Hester Burton, John Murray, 1949.

83 George Eliot's residence, North Bank, St John's Wood; known as the Priory. Photo Radio Times Hulton Picture Library.

84 Drawing-room of the Priory. Engraving from Cross's *Life of George Eliot*, 1885.

Titian's *The Tribute Money*; oil. Staatliche Kunstsammlungen, Dresden.

85 Titian's *Annunciation*; oil. Scuola di San Rocco, Venice. Photo Osvaldo Böhm.

86 Reading-lamp said to have belonged to George Eliot. Coventry City Libraries. Photo Eileen Tweedy.

87 Stationery cabinet said to have belonged to George Eliot. Coventry City Libraries. Photo Eileen Tweedy.

88 George Eliot; preliminary sketch for the portrait painted in 1860 by Samuel Laurence. Girton College Library, Cambridge. Photo Edward Leigh.

89 Barbara Bodichon; portrait by unknown artist. Girton College Library, Cambridge. Photo Edward Leigh.

91 George Eliot wearing a mantilla; etching by S. Schoff. Photo Mansell Collection.

93 Dorothea Casaubon finds her husband dead in the garden, from an original by W.L. Taylor, 1886. From *Scenes and Characters from the Works of George Eliot*, edition de luxe, volume II, 1888.

94 Eliza Lynn Linton. Photo Radio Times Hulton Picture Library.

96 George Eliot; pencil drawing by Lady Alma Tadema, 21 March 1877. National Portrait Gallery, London.

97 G.H. Lewes; pencil drawing by Rudolph Lehmann, 20 June 1867. British Museum, Department of Prints and Drawings. Photo Eileen Tweedy.

98 George Eliot; portrait by George du Maurier. From *George du Maurier* by Leonée Ormond, 1969.

101 Dante; watercolour by Sir Frederic William Burton, presented by the artist to the Leweses in October 1864. Nuneaton Library. Photo Eileen Tweedy.

Carved oak knee writing-board, stamped 'Elma Stuart fecit'. Coventry City Libraries. Photo Eileen Tweedy.

102 Meeting held for Women's Suffrage; from *Our Mothers*, edited by Alan Bott, text by Irene Clephane, 1932.

103 The Ludwig's Well at Bad Homburg; woodcut, 1850. Staatsbibliothek, Berlin.

105 The old synagogue, Frankfurt; engraving by W. Lang after the drawing by J.S. Dielmann, *c.* 1850. Stadt-und-Universitätsbibliothek, Frankfurt-am-Main.

First page of the manuscript of *Daniel Deronda*. British Museum, Department of Manuscripts. MS Add 34039, folio 3.

106 Maxstoke Priory; details of shields on the ceiling. By kind permission of Mr and Mrs R. Tyacke. Photo Eric G. Miller.

107 George Eliot; drawing by Princess Louise on a programme of a concert at St James's Hall, 16 March 1877. By courtesy of Professor Haight.

108 The Heights, Witley, near Haslemere. Photo Radio Times Hulton Picture Library.

109 George Henry Lewes's tombstone in Highgate Cemetery. Photo Eileen Tweedy.

110 Inscribed copy to Caroline Bray of *The Impressions of Theophrastus Such*; 'Eastbourne, 29 May 1879'. Coventry City Libraries.

113 No. 4 Cheyne Walk, Chelsea. Photo Radio Times Hulton Picture Library.

115 Isaac Evans. Nuneaton Library. Photo Eileen Tweedy.

116 George Eliot's tomb in Highgate Cemetery. Photo Eileen Tweedy.

BIBLIOGRAPHICAL NOTE

No one can now write on George Eliot's life without extreme indebtedness to the magnificent biographical works of G. S. Haight: in particular, his *George Eliot and John Chapman* (1940), his seven-volume edition (to which an eighth is shortly to be added) of *The George Eliot Letters* (1954–55); and his *George Eliot: A Biography* (1968).

Of other lives of George Eliot, I have used those by J. W. Cross (*George Eliot's Life as related in her letters and Journals*: 1885); by Mathilde Blind (*George Eliot*: 1883); by Oscar Browning (*Life of George Eliot*: 1890); by Elizabeth S. Haldane (*George Eliot and her Times*: 1927); and by Anne Fremantle (*George Eliot*: 1933). Joan Bennett's *George Eliot: Her mind and her art* (1948) contains an outline of the life, but its outstanding value is its literary criticism.

Useful books relating to George Eliot's early life are: *Seth Bede, 'the Methody'; his life and labours: chiefly written by himself* (1859); *George Eliot in Derbyshire*, by 'Guy Roslyn' (1876); *Phases of Opinion and Experience during a Long Life*, by Charles Bray (1884); *The Cheverels of Cheverel Manor*, by Lady Newdigate-Newdegate (1898); *The True Story of George Eliot* by William Mottram (1905) – he was a cousin on the Evans' side, and prints many interesting photographs; and *George Eliot: Scenes and People in her Novels*, by Charles S. Olcott (1911). Also helpful in this context are many of the pamphlets emanating from Warwickshire about various aspects, principally local, of George Eliot's life, and also some of the pamphlets written as guide-books to places incidentally associated with her, notably *Chilvers Coton Parish Church Guide* by Dorothy Dodds, *Arbury Hall* by Gordon Nares (1953), and the *History of Capesthorne* by Letitia Bromley Davenport.

For the later life, K. A. MacKenzie's *Edith Simcox and George Eliot* (1961) is indispensable. Anna I. Kitchel's *George Lewes and George Eliot* (1933) is helpful in relation to the Lewes family. References to George Eliot can be found in the memoirs of most people who had any contact with her. Those I have principally cited are: *My Literary Life in London* by Mrs Lynn Linton (1899), together with *Mrs Lynn Linton* by George Somes Layard (1901); *The Middle Years* by Henry James (1917); *A Writer's Recollections* by Mrs Humphry Ward (1918); *Aspects and Impressions* by Edmund Gosse (1922); I have also used *Barbara Bodichon, 1827–1891* by Hester Burton (1949) – a new life is needed; *I, too, have lived in Arcadia* by Mrs Belloc Lowndes (1941) and *Diaries and letters of Marie Belloc Lowndes, 1911–1947* edited by Susan Lowndes (1971).

Virginia Woolf's essay on George Eliot is reprinted in *The Common Reader* (First Series; 1925). The other critical works mentioned are F. R. Leavis's essay in his *The Great Tradition* (1948), and Joan Bennett's book referred to above. In this field an essential book is *George Eliot: The Critical Heritage* edited by David Carroll (1971).

ACKNOWLEDGMENTS

I must express my thanks to Her Majesty the Queen for her gracious permission to quote from the letters of Queen Victoria; and to Mr Robert Mackworth-Young, Librarian at Windsor Castle, for looking out relevant passages for me.

My warm thanks for companionable help and encouragement are due to Nuala O'Faolain, to whom this book is dedicated: to Professor G. S. Haight for the utmost generosity and critical kindness; to Mr Stanley Baron of Thames and Hudson who will provide for this book, as he did for my last, all the constructive help one could ask for from an editor; to Miss Erica Gentle, of Thames and Hudson, for her search for illustrations; to Mr Harold Rubinstein for information about Halcott Glover; to Miss Maria Rawlinson for her patient tracking down of wills, and to the many people who helped me in George Eliot's country and in neighbourhoods associated with her, especially: Mrs K. M. Adams of Coventry; the Reverend Thomas Ashworth, of Ellastone, Staffs.; Mr S. H. Barlow, Borough Librarian of Nuneaton; Lady Bromley Davenport, of Capesthorne, Cheshire; Canon F. S. Herbert, of Nuneaton; Mrs. Rachel Jones, of Hill Wootton, Warwickshire; the Reverend M. W. Mansbridge, of Chilvers Coton and Astley; the Hon. Mrs FitzRoy Newdegate, of Arbury Hall, Warwickshire.

GEORGE ELIOT'S WORKS

INDEX

Figures in italic refer to illustrations; a textural reference may also appear on the illustration page.
George Eliot herself is omitted from this index; works and publications of whatever length are in italics; dates are appended where they may prevent confusion. In general, titles conferred after 1880 are omitted; so are people and places only glancingly referred to.